QUEEN MARY

Her Life and Times

H.M. QUEEN MARY

A formal study of Queen Mary when Queen Mother.

QUEEN MARY

Her Life and Times

By

MARGUERITE D. PEACOCKE

ODHAMS PRESS LIMITED
LONG ACRE, LONDON

COLOUR PLATES

MADE AND PRINTED IN GREAT BRITAIN
BY ODHAMS (WATFORD) LIMITED, WATFORD
S.353.S.

CONTENTS

THE FUTURE QUEEN CONSORT
A charming study of Queen Mary, then the young and gracious Duchess of York.

FROM GIRLHOOD
TO QUEEN

The life of Queen Mary, the most universally beloved and revered woman in the world today, presents an unparalleled link between the past and future history of Britain. Her great-grandfather, George III—whom she never saw but of whom she delighted to learn, at first-hand, from her maternal grandmother, the Duchess of Cambridge, who was his daughter-in-law—ascended the throne nearly two hundred years ago. Her great-grandson, Charles, Duke of Cornwall, whose early progress she watches with such joy and interest, may well be reigning long after the present century has run its course.

The Queen's grandmother has not merely lived through those eighty-five years which for all but the very oldest of us constitute all that we have ever known as "our own times," she has served each generation from her own to that of her contemporaries' great-grandchildren. She has not only seen history in the making, she has helped to make it.

As Princess May of Teck, Queen Mary was born to a place, if a remote one, in the line of succession. Her mother, Princess Mary of Cambridge by birth and Duchess of Teck by marriage, was the only first cousin of Queen Victoria (herself an only child) who possessed British-born heirs. It was in recognition of this proximity to the Crown that Queen Victoria granted the newly-wed Duchess of Teck and her husband the tenancy of the Kensington Palace apartments in which she herself had lived until her accession. The ground-floor room in which the future Queen Regnant had been born on 24 May, 1819, became the Teck family dining-room. The old "nursery suite," as it is called to this day, on the floor above, became on 26 May, 1867, the birthplace of the future Queen Consort.

The new Princess of Teck was christened Victoria Mary Augusta Louisa Olga Pauline Claudine Agnes, in honour of a large number of royal relatives on both sides. Officially she was known, for brevity, as Princess Victoria Mary. In private her name was still further abbreviated; her family, her intimate friends, and in later years her husband, simply called her May, and thus she soon acquired the affectionate if unofficial title of Princess May.

The world into which Princess May of Teck arrived was not so very different from that into which Queen Victoria had been born forty-eight years previously. Time marched more slowly in that mid-nineteenth-century era than it does today. The "electric telegraph" had come, but not the telephone, and gas was still the most

THE HAPPY FAMILY OF TECK

The Duchess of Teck with Princess May and two of her brothers.

up-to-date form of illumination. There were railway trains but no motor-cars, although that year of 1867 saw one notable contribution towards more speedy progress—the bicycle. Much of what we now call the classics was then modern literature; Lord Tennyson was Poet Laureate, Charles Dickens was still alive, and so was Thomas Carlyle. Many of the great events which now fill pages of our history books belonged then to a still unknown future.

But the world was nevertheless rapidly developing into something like the world we know today. The Education Act making it compulsory for every child in Britain to go to school was passed during those years when little Princess May, her fair hair cut in a fringe in front and tied in a bow at the back, sat doing her lessons at the dainty little walnut and ormolu desk with its blue velvet top and three tiny drawers which was the gift of her mother and which can still be seen today in the old Kensington Palace nursery. In those years, too, bank holidays were introduced and trade unions officially recognized. In days to come the little Princess was to take the deepest interest in these and many other social changes which affected the lives of the people who were to acclaim her as the First Lady in their land. Meantime, she enjoyed a simple but fascinating childhood.

It seems odd, and somehow rather encouraging, to learn that Princess May, who was to grow into a woman of such unrivalled grace, was once regarded as something of a tomboy. It explains perhaps the warm humanity which was always to be found, by those who sought or needed it, behind the outward dignity of mien. She was the eldest of the family and she never had a sister, just three handsome, adventurous brothers, of whom Prince Alexander, now the Earl of Athlone and always "Alge" to his family, alone survives. Princess May also spent many happy hours playing with her young cousins, the "Waleses," children of the future Edward VII, then Prince of Wales, one of whom was one day to become her husband. But if boys were her favourite playmates, she had at least one taste in common with most small girls: she loved dolls, and at eighty-five she loves them still.

Many of the tastes which Queen Mary was to develop in later life had their origins in her earliest years. As a baby in arms she was taken right across Europe on a round of family visits, and this was followed by many more childhood journeyings. As a result she came to look upon travel as not only one of the greatest pleasures in life, but also the greatest education in the world. She often visited her grandmother, the old Duchess of Cambridge, at Cambridge Cottage, Kew. Now this old family home is no longer a royal residence, but part of the administrative offices. However, Queen Mary has rarely missed making at least an annual visit to Kew Gardens to see the flowers and trees which she remembers from childhood, and to seek out, with that tireless zeal which has always spurred her in search of new knowledge, any fresh acquisitions.

Those long-ago visits to Kew were made partly to delight her grandmother and partly so that Princess May might benefit from what was then regarded as being almost

9

H.R.H. PRINCESS MAY

From a portrait by G. Koberwein in 1872.

"country" air. Strangely enough, the woman who in later life was scarcely to know a day's illness was in childhood accounted delicate. Once indeed she was so ill that her parents feared for her life. The dangerous fever which happily passed with almost the same suddenness as it had come was attributed to the unwholesome atmosphere arising from the Round Pond in Kensington Gardens, which can still be seen from her old home.

By the time that she was in her third year, Princess May's family also possessed a country home, White Lodge, Richmond, whose surroundings, pleasant as they are today, were then considerably more rural. The house, with its lovely garden, was, like the Kensington Palace apartments, put at the disposal of the Duke and Duchess of Teck by Queen Victoria.

Growing up so close to the throne, Princess May must have received an early initiation into the state and ceremony of royal life. Her parents attended all the usual state functions. They entertained many illustrious guests. They stayed in many of the stateliest homes in Britain and visited the Queen at Windsor Castle and at Balmoral. The little Princess herself was frequently seen and admired by Queen Victoria, who, although normally absorbed mainly in her many direct descendants, favoured this young cousin with a singular degree of affectionate interest.

Yet, despite all this, the future Queen Mary had a very simple upbringing. Her parents were known among all their wide circle of friends for their complete devotion to each other, to their children and to their home. They had a great love of "cosiness." When they planned to give a party, using for their receptions the famous Council Room in which Queen Victoria had held her first Privy Council, the plump and supremely domesticated Duchess of Teck would put on a large apron and help to prepare the room for her guests.

In such a homely atmosphere Princess May was naturally brought up to do things for herself and to make herself useful. She became as expert at stitching red-flannel petticoats as at fine embroidery. She was equally used to her mother's visitors being among the most distinguished persons in Europe as to finding that the Duchess was receiving some distressed parishioner who had come to her for help. In an age when many children saw little of their parents, being largely left to the care of nurses and governesses, Princess May and her brothers were constantly with their mother and father. The Duchess gave them their first Bible lessons. The Duke taught them the names of flowers and trees and how to recognize the wild birds and woodland animals.

Queen Mary's family was never rich. Her mother possessed some interesting heirlooms, but no private fortune. Her father, the Duke of Teck, was the son of a morganatic marriage and had no inheritance of either land or wealth. His title was not hereditary, but was bestowed upon him by his kinsman, the King of Württemberg (the princely House of Teck, dating from the twelfth century and taking its name from a feudal castle, having been absorbed into the Württemberg line). His father, Prince Alexander of Württemberg, had renounced his place in the line of succession to his country's throne in order to marry Countess Claudia Rhédey, a woman of beauty and ancient Hungarian lineage, although not of royal birth. While on her mother's side Queen Mary descends from the long line of English kings dating back to William the Conqueror, it is through her father that she can claim kinship with St. Stephen of Hungary, with the famous ruling House of Hapsburg, with a great dynasty of kings of Poland and with many other illustrious royal and imperial families.

It has often been said that it was to her Hungarian ancestry that Queen Mary owed her passionate love of colour and beauty. It may be equally true to say that it was from her Württemberg forebears that she inherited at least some of her practical determination to leave the world a better place than she found it. For the small, cultured and highly progressive kingdom of Württemberg (since incorporated first into the Empire and then into the Republic of Germany) had long ago introduced much of the social legislation which is now associated with the idea of the welfare state. It was a far-seeing ruler of Württemberg who issued the surprising but eminently sensible decree that each newly-married couple should plant two fruit trees to celebrate their wedding, thus laying the foundation of a prosperous fruit-growing industry which in turn formed the basis of a

THE LITTLE PRINCESS
Queen Mary at the age of six.

11

thoroughly sound national economy.

When Princess May was in her seventeenth year her parents found that the upkeep of their Palace home was beyond their means. Although their personal tastes were never extravagant, they had carried on the old tradition of keeping "open house" and they were immensely generous both in dispensing private charity and in supporting the many good causes in which they took an active interest. For nearly two years they left England for a more retired and economical life on the Continent, where they were able to live as private residents instead of as royalty.

For Princess May the exile thus forced upon her by family circumstances was to provide many wonderful opportunities which she would otherwise never have known had she enjoyed the more conventional preparation for emergence into late-nineteenth-century London Society. Unlike previous holidays abroad, her stay on the Continent was not confined to visits to relatives. Her family spent some of the time in small private hotels and the rest in a furnished villa in Italy. Princess May enjoyed—and endured— much the same experiences as any other girl of her age travelling abroad with cultured parents of moderate means. The usual privileges accorded to royalty were lacking. Like most English travellers she found hotel dining-rooms stuffy, contrived with difficulty to persuade someone to open a window and watched with annoyance when some less hardy guest insisted on its being closed.

The Princess by no means lived the life of a recluse. She met many of her mother's friends and was in turn received by them. But during these months she enjoyed a freedom from much of the formality which was, inevitably, to surround her in later years. The first "grown-up" dance which she attended, for instance, was held not in a Palace, but at a British Consulate. Moreover, social functions played a very small part in her life. She visited churches, museums and galleries, listening with something far beyond the tourist's casual attention while their custodians expounded on the treasures to be found therein. She visited Dante's birthplace (on the six hundred and twentieth anniversary of his birth), examined early editions of his works and went on to see the little church

QUEEN MARY WITH HER BROTHERS

Princess May of Teck at tea with her brothers, Prince Adolphus, Prince Francis and, seated, Prince Alexander, now the Earl of Athlone.

NINETEEN YEARS OLD

Princess May in her "coming-out" gown.

where he was married. During a visit to Switzerland she scrambled up rocky paths the better to appreciate the grandeur of the scenery, rose before dawn to witness the great spectacle of the sunrise in the mountains and made expeditions on the lakes in small, uncomfortable boats, all of which activities denoted a remarkable degree of fortitude and enterprise in a young girl of the late 1880s. For her the prolonged family "holiday" became an extensive educational tour.

So vividly did her experiences live in her mind, and so enthusiastic was she in recounting them to her grandchildren in years to come, that more than half a century later Princess Margaret was to set out on her own much shorter tour of Italy determined to see for herself at least some of the fascinating and beautiful things which had delighted her grandmother so much.

Finally, the Teck family returned to England, via Paris. With much sadness the Kensington Palace apartments were relinquished and their cherished belongings were somehow fitted into White Lodge. This remained Queen Mary's only permanent home until her marriage, although various town houses were put at her mother's disposal by friends for temporary occupation.

Thus it was from a house in Chester Square that Princess May eventually made her entrance into London Society. When at the age of nineteen she was presented at Court she made her curtsey to the Queen not with other débutantes, but in the privacy of the Royal Closet at Buckingham Palace, this privilege being accorded owing to her close relationship to the sovereign.

At White Lodge the Princess quietly pursued her education at an age when most of her contemporaries considered that they had acquired quite as much learning as they would ever require. But the Princess was inspired by that same thirst for knowledge which was sending the pioneers of higher education for women to battle their way

PRINCESS MAY

A formal study of the quiet, gracious girl destined to a lifetime of service to her country.

QUEEN-TO-BE

The serene and beautiful young Princess.

through the universities. She was already a good linguist, speaking, reading and writing French, German and Italian. She possessed the usual accomplishments—music, art, dancing and sewing. But the standards which she set herself were so high that she considered these to be merely the beginning.

She now devoted herself to reading, not in a desultory way to pass the time, but in accordance with a definite plan. Her former governess, the tall, dark Madame Bricka, of Alsatian origin and strong radical outlook, remained as her companion and ally in the constant struggle to find time for more serious studies without neglecting any of the duties which fell to the Princess as her mother's only daughter. The family circle was already growing smaller. Princess May's eldest brother, Prince Adolphus, joined the Army and was posted to India. The second brother, Prince Francis, also became a soldier, and the youngest member of the family, now the Earl of Athlone, eventually adopted a military career, so that all three sons followed in their father's footsteps. Their grandmother, the old Duchess of Cambridge, who had done so much to awaken Princess May's deep love and reverence for the past, died in 1889, having remembered in her will to bequeath a "wedding present" to her granddaughter.

It was, however, not until December, 1891, when Princess May was in her twenty-fifth year, that she became betrothed to the ultimate heir to the throne, Prince Albert Victor, Duke of Clarence, the eldest son of the then Prince of Wales. The nation rejoiced at the prospect of having, for the first time since the sixteenth century, a British-born Queen Consort. The engagement, as always in the case of royalty, was to be a short one, and when the two families gathered at Sandringham, early in January, 1892, it was with the two-fold purpose of celebrating the betrothal and planning the wedding. When the Princess and her fellow-guests arrived they found that the prospective bridegroom had fallen a victim to the influenza epidemic which was then sweeping the country. Although at first his illness was not regarded as serious, within a few days it proved fatal. St. George's Chapel at Windsor, where arrangements were

PRINCESS MAY OF TECK
A coloured photograph of Queen Mary as a girl.

JUBILEE THANKSGIVING SERVICE

This painting by Frank O. Salisbury shows King George V and Queen Mary being received by the Archbishop of Canterbury at the West Door of St. Paul's Cathedral. Many members of the Royal Family were present; also foreign royalty, high-ranking clergy, members of the nobility and the Lord Mayor of London.

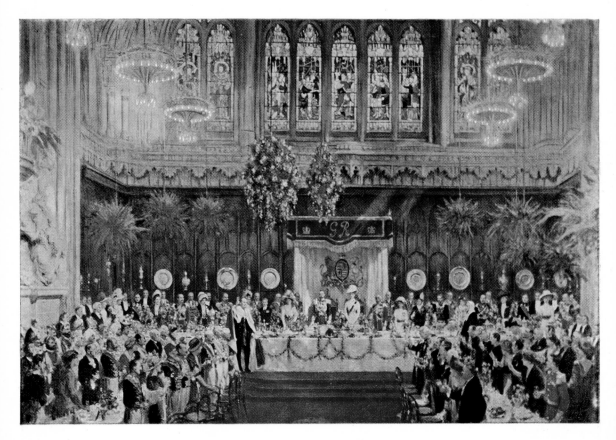

CORONATION LUNCH AT THE GUILDHALL

King George V and Queen Mary at the Guildhall in 1911; a painting by Solomon J. Solomon.

A ROYAL GROUP

King George V, Queen Mary, Prince Edward and Princess Mary; a painting by J. Lavery.

QUEEN MARY WITH PRINCE CHARLES

Queen Mary at the Christening of Prince Charles.

ROYAL BETROTHAL

Princess May photographed with the Duke of Clarence shortly before his tragic death.

THE FUTURE DUCHESS OF YORK

After a year's retirement from public life the young Princess May became engaged to the Duke of York.
This photograph was taken shortly before their marriage in July, 1893.

being made for the marriage, was instead prepared for the young Prince's funeral.

For more than a year Princess May retired from public life, spending part of the time staying with old family friends at home and on the Continent. When she returned it was to receive a proposal from that other playmate of her earliest years, Prince George of Wales, Duke of York, who had succeeded his brother as the ultimate heir to the throne.

Their wedding took place on 6 July, 1893, in the Chapel Royal, St. James's, where Queen Victoria and Prince Albert had been married more than half a century before. The ten bridesmaids were all Princesses, cousins in some degree of both the bride and bridegroom. The trousseau was, down to the last detail, of British manufacture. The Princess was married from Buckingham Palace, which was one day to be her home as Queen, and it was there that the reception was held, the newly-married Duke and Duchess of York appearing on the balcony before leaving for their honeymoon at Sandringham.

Their first London residence was York House, St. James's Palace, while the country home of the future King George V and Queen Mary was York Cottage, a modest and even cramped residence for the growing family with which they were soon to be blessed, but a real home, and distinguished visitors never failed to be impressed by the air of cosy domesticity pervading its small, simply furnished rooms.

The praise which Queen Victoria lavished upon her grandson's bride makes almost depressing reading with its constant stress on the new Duchess of York's complete lack

THE ROYAL WEDDING

The Duke and Duchess of York with their bridesmaids, each of whom was a royal princess.

THE DUCHESS AT HOME

At work at her desk at Sandringham.

of "frivolity." But there was much wisdom in the joy with which the old Queen welcomed the advent of this young couple who were to set an example, as she put it, of a "quiet, steady life" and whose home was to be supervised by a wife and mother so completely "unfrivolous." The survival of British family life through those legendary "naughty 'nineties," those proverbially gay Edwardian days, and the even more difficult and disturbed years which followed, was to owe much to the leadership of the woman who, first as Duchess of York, then as Princess of Wales, and finally as Queen, was to place the love of home, husband and children second only to the service of the great family of the commonwealth of nations and above all other personal considerations, whatever the sacrifice.

Not one of her children was born in a palace. For the birthplace of her first child the Duchess of York chose White Lodge, her old girlhood home. There the birth of the future Edward VIII took place on 23 June, 1894, under the capable supervision of her mother and with the minimum of fuss and ceremony. The following month, in the family drawing-room at Richmond, an illustrious gathering of royalties and statesmen met for the christening, at which the then Archbishop of Canterbury used the famous silver-gilt font brought from Windsor Castle for the occasion.

The next year a second son, the late King, was born on 14 December, the anniversary of the death of the Prince Consort, a circumstance which greatly endeared him to Queen Victoria and also ensured that the name of Albert should stand first at his christening. Like his sister and younger brothers, he was born at York Cottage and baptized in the small church of St. Mary Magdalene on the Sandringham estate.

To mark the Diamond Jubilee of 1897, the Duke and Duchess of York, already the parents of three children (the present Princess Royal was born in the spring of that year), paid a three weeks' official visit to Ireland. This was a triumphant success, despite early misgivings on account of the strong political feelings prevailing, and was the forerunner of other tours which were to do so much to endear King George V and Queen Mary to the hearts of their subjects throughout the Empire.

QUEEN VICTORIA WITH THE DUKE AND DUCHESS OF YORK

The Duke of York with his young wife and his grandmother, between whom there existed a bond of mutual affection and admiration.

The year, however, ended sadly, for in October the Duchess of Teck died as the result of a second operation following upon one performed some months earlier. Three years later came the death of the Duke of Teck, who never fully recovered from the shock of losing his devoted wife. This was a time of great anxiety as well as mourning for the Duchess of York, whose three brothers were all on active service in the Boer War. Then, in January, 1901, came the death of Queen Victoria.

It was decided that despite the family mourning the Duke and Duchess of York should carry out the great Empire tour which had already been planned for them, and that during their travels they should still be known by the name by which they were already so familiar rather than as Prince and Princess of Wales, the titles so long associated with the Duke of York's parents. The eldest son of the Sovereign, however, automatically succeeds to the title of Duke of Cornwall, and so it was as the Duke and Duchess of Cornwall and York that the royal travellers set forth on their seven and a half months' tour. Like their son and daughter-in-law and their granddaughter and her husband in the years to come they faced a long parting from their children. The faithful Madame Bricka was left to watch over the nursery.

The royal party sailed in H.M.S. *Ophir*, whose crew, by special dispensation, included one woman, the laundryman being allowed to take his wife, since he declared himself incapable of the elaborate starching which the fashions of the day made necessary for the Duchess and her ladies. For the Duchess of Cornwall and York the voyage was a considerable ordeal, for, although an experienced traveller, Queen Mary has never been an enthusiastic sailor, while she has always disliked extreme heat. Among her compensations was the fact that her youngest brother was a member of her husband's suite.

The tour was a great test of physical endurance, for on the way to Australia there were stops at Gibraltar, Malta, Aden, Ceylon and Singapore. On the voyage the Duchess became the first British Princess to submit to the ministrations of Father Neptune in the traditional ceremony of Crossing the Line. The most important single event was the opening by the Duke of the Federal Parliament, which marked the birth of the Commonwealth of Australia, when the Duchess pressed a golden button which released the news to the world. They went on to New Zealand and returned to England by way of South Africa and Canada.

King Edward VII then created his son Prince of Wales, and for nearly nine years the future Queen Mary bore the title of Princess of Wales. The family moved to Marlborough House, the London residence traditionally reserved for Queens Dowager or heirs-apparent. The small cottage at Sandringham remained their country home and it was there that the late Duke of Kent was born in December, 1902, while 1905 saw the birth of their youngest child, Prince John, who was unhappily always delicate and died at the early age of thirteen.

The Princess of Wales still remained in the closest touch with her own family,

QUEEN MARY WITH HER FIRST SON

The Duke and Duchess of York, now proud young parents, photographed with their first child **at** *White Lodge, Richmond, in 1894.*

which by now included a number of nephews and nieces. Her second brother, who died in 1910, remained a bachelor, but Prince Adolphus, later the Marquess of Cambridge, married the daughter of the first Duke of Westminster and had two sons and two daughters, while Prince Alexander, now the Earl of Athlone, who married his cousin, the former Princess Alice of Albany, had a son and a daughter.

Somehow the Princess of Wales contrived to combine this very full family life with the ever-growing burden of official duties which fell to her as the wife of the heir to the throne. In the spring of 1904 she and her husband paid a State visit to Vienna. They went on to Württemberg. Queen Mary always retained a great affection for her father's native land, and when a few years later she became Queen she quartered the Württemberg arms on her own coat-of-arms and adopted the national colour for the badges which she gave to her ladies-in-waiting.

In the autumn of 1905 the Prince and Princess of Wales again set forth on a long voyage, this time to visit India. Wherever the royal party went the same round of functions confronted them: Durbar, garden party, banquet, review, reception; a strenuous programme even in a climate less trying to Western visitors. Day after day the Princess and her husband took their places upon the crimson thrones beneath canopies of cloth of gold, to receive homage from the endless procession of richly jewelled potentates staggering under the weight of their ceremonial dress against a

QUEEN MARY
AND FAMILY
Left to right: *Queen Mary; Prince Henry (Duke of Gloucester); Prince George (late Duke of Kent); Princess Mary (Princess Royal); Prince Edward (now Duke of Windsor); Prince John; Prince Albert (late George VI). This family group was photographed at Abergeldie in 1906.*

background of exotic pageantry enlivened by the inevitable parade of elephants.

The Princess's exquisite regard for the feelings of others and for their traditional observances, however odd and inconvenient these might seem to a stranger like herself, caused her to submit to many experiences which, although intended to do her honour, must have been considerable ordeals.

On her previous Empire tour she had, despite the intense heat, cheerfully enveloped herself for a few moments in a vast ostrich boa, to the delight of the donor from whose hand she had just received it, and donned the cumbersome and far from elegant Kiwi "mat" in order to appear among the Maoris dressed as befitted her high rank. So in India she submitted with calm dignity to the long symbolic ceremonial tribute of Parsee women. Various tokens of prosperity—eggs, nuts and water—were one by one passed seven times round her head while rice and nuts were showered over her. Before the tour was over she even knew, from more than one experience, what it was to ride upon an elephant.

Amidst this lavish display of Oriental wealth and magnificence, the Princess was deeply moved by the terrible signs of poverty which could not be concealed from her penetrating gaze. It was she who suggested that, as some slight gesture of sympathy, the traditional tributes of fruit and other foodstuffs offered to the royal visitors should be distributed among the poor.

Not long after their return to England the Prince and Princess of Wales visited Madrid to attend the wedding of the then King Alfonso to their cousin, Princess Ena, who had been one of the Princess's child bridesmaids. In 1908 they paid a private visit to Paris, travelling as Lord and Lady Killarney. They visited friends, went to the Opera and spent long days sight-seeing, just like any other tourists, although the Princess of Wales firmly refused to buy any clothes in the traditional home of fashion, politely saying that the fittings would take up too much of her time, but actually determined that her own countrymen should not be deprived of her custom.

The time was, however, coming when there would be no more opportunities for holidays abroad and even many of the official visits overseas would be delegated to other members of the family. On 6 May, 1910, King Edward VII died at Buckingham Palace; the Prince of Wales acceded to the throne and his wife became Queen. Her first act was to omit the name of Victoria from her signature so that she would be known simply as "Queen Mary." She signed herself "Mary R," and by adding the royal "R" after her name established a precedent which has since been followed by the present Queen Mother, Queen Elizabeth. It was a small but significant gesture. So many Queens Consort had been shadowy figures whose very names are not easily remembered by successive generations. Queen Mary was to take her place as First Lady in the Land in no mere nominal sense. She was to share in the fullest degree in her husband's leadership of his people.

H.M. QUEEN MARY

A studio portrait of her as Queen Consort.

PUBLIC LIFE AS QUEEN

*I*f future generations should revert to the ancient practice of surnaming kings and queens according to their outstanding qualities, the Consort of King George V would surely go down to history as Queen Mary the Regal. For many people the name of the first Queen who ever lived to see her grand-daughter ascend the throne of Britain will always bring to mind a vision of her as she appeared on some great State occasion, decked in the full splendour of her ceremonial array. She is one of the last women in the world today who can wear a profusion of diamonds, from the crown on her head to the rings on her fingers, in the old grand manner of other days.

Queen Mary had barely crossed the threshold of middle age when her name became a by-word, standing equally for all that was most correct in conduct and all that was most majestic in mien, in an era in which rectitude was becoming unfashionable and majesty was rapidly passing away. State appearances, important and impressive as they were, represented but one limited aspect of her public life, but she was always regal. Wherever she went, whatever she did, in the mourning which she was destined to wear so many times in her long life, in the simple, if elegant, dress of every day, even in the privacy of her own home, she always looked a queen. Yet she could never be mistaken for a mere figurehead of royalty. She also was, and looked, a great woman, in heart and mind and spirit, and in that supreme attribute of true greatness, her personal humility.

Her first public appearance as Queen was, inevitably, as a heavily-veiled royal mourner at the funeral of her father-in-law, King Edward VII. In the midst of those sad traditional rites the new Queen's warm humanity was already to be seen. By her own desire she took, for the last time in her married life, second place, and in the St. George's Chapel at Windsor it was the widowed Queen Mother Alexandra who stood beside King George V as his father was laid to rest.

The etiquette of the day prescribed a full twelve months of court mourning. Thus one of the first portraits for which Queen Mary posed after her accession was also one of the few which portrayed her in black, a colour which she never wore from choice. It showed her dressed as she had been for the first State Opening of Parliament of the new reign, her sombre attire enlivened by the blue ribbon of the Garter which her husband had conferred upon her soon after he came to the throne.

Then, on 22 June, 1911, came Coronation Day, the greatest of all the State

THE NEWLY-CROWNED KING AND QUEEN
King George V and his Consort, Queen Mary, on their Coronation day.

ceremonies in which Queen Mary was ever to take part as a central figure. With the crowning of King George V and his Consort, the centuries-old coronation ritual was once again restored to its rightful place as a religious service and not merely as a picturesque formality and the occasion of high secular festival. Queen Mary, like her husband, regarded the solemn ceremony in Westminster Abbey as the final consecration of her life to the service of her people. Her devotion to the Christian religion has been as uncompromising as it has been unostentatious, and the example which she has set as a practising churchwoman is not the least of her contributions to the life of the nation. She can recall the Sundays on which she has missed attending church, because her rare absences have all been due to the most exceptional circumstances. When living at Buckingham Palace she visited the private chapel at least once every day. Accepting the fact that opinions varied as to the correct observance of the Sabbath she herself did nothing which could offend any school of thought. If there was ever dancing or other entertainment in the royal homes on a Saturday, it always ended—as it still does—by midnight. If she has taken advantage of a quiet Sunday afternoon to pay a private visit to an exhibition, she has never bought anything, but returned on a week-day to make her purchases. She has undertaken her spiritual obligations as a godmother with as much responsibility as she faced her duties as a parent.

On the night of the Coronation King George V, faithful to his lifelong habit of recording the day's events before retiring to his rest, wrote in his diary: "Darling May looked lovely, and it was indeed a comfort to me to have her by my side, as she has

CORONATION CELEBRATIONS—SECOND DAY
The royal coach halts at Temple Bar.

ever been to me during these last eighteen years." For ten minutes after returning to Buckingham Palace from the long and exhausting Coronation ceremony, the newly-crowned Queen had stood beside the King on the crimson-draped balcony to acknowledge the cheers of the crowds which packed the whole length of the Mall. Next day a State drive through London enabled yet more thousands to see the new Sovereign and his Consort. Then the climax to the Coronation ceremonies came in an unexpected and brilliantly imaginative project in whose planning Queen Mary played as great a part as her husband. This was the visit to India for the Delhi Durbar in 1911, when, for the first time in history, a British Queen travelled beyond the confines of the continent of Europe. Once again Queen Mary, in the course of duty, had to face her old enemies, the stormy sea and the burning heat, but to her great delight her eldest brother, who had succeeded their father as Duke of Teck, accompanied the royal party as A.D.C.

Indians, in whose eyes the most magnificent British uniforms paled before the dazzling splendour of their own ceremonial attire, were not greatly impressed by the outward appearance of the male members of the party, but all were loud in their acclamation of their "Great White Empress." Queen Mary, her lovely hair still golden, dressed in white, cream or her favourite pale blue, except when she wore her gold Coronation gown, with her colourful regalia and her sparkling jewels, left an undying memory.

The Queen, determined that, despite the heat and the strange surroundings, the Durbar ceremonies should be unmarred by the slightest hitch, insisted that at the rehearsal both she and the King should play their own "parts" and not be represented by proxies in order to spare themselves fatigue. But there was one incident during the investiture which was unrehearsed and called for an unforgettable demonstration of Queen Mary's high courage and perfect composure. When some of the tents caught fire and shouts of "Fire" were heard from all sides, she sat very pale but perfectly still, while her husband continued to pin on decorations as though nothing untoward were happening. Later it was learnt that there had been a serious risk that the King and Queen and hundreds of their subjects would be burnt to death. There were many tributes to the Queen's calmness that day, but few of those who praised her knew that she—who was so singularly free from fanciful fears—had always dreaded fire.

Queen Mary's contribution to the grace and dignity of State occasions is not limited to her own regal appearance. She loves and respects royal pageantry, not as an idle show, but as part of the tradition of the Monarchy and of Britain. In her zeal to preserve the full significance of ceremonial she has studied every aspect of the subject in all its intricate detail, so that when some point of doubt has arisen even the experts have deferred to her ruling, and foreign courts have often sought her guidance.

She has always been quick to note and reprove any careless omission of correct observance. A decoration wrongly worn annoys her intensely, and her vigilance never

DELHI DURBAR—1911

King George V and Queen Mary, in their State robes, leave the dais after the crowning ceremony.

THE FAMILIAR TOQUE

Queen Mary in happy mood at a Balmoral garden fête.

fails. Once, in her eighties, she was driving past the London headquarters of a royal institution and noticed that, although it was one of the officially appointed days for the flying of flags, the mast was bare. On her return to Marlborough House she ordered a telephone inquiry to be made to ascertain the reason for the absence of the flag. As she had anticipated, the officials had overlooked the date. Queen Mary never overlooks anything.

Throughout her long public life Queen Mary, despite her personal shyness and genuine humility, has never failed to appreciate the pleasure which her own appearances and those of other members of her family give to millions of people to whom even the sight of royalty is by no means an everyday occurrence. Even her choice of millinery was dictated by her understanding of other people's natural desire to study the expressions and features of royal visitors. From the time that she became Queen she adhered faithfully to her famous toques, rejecting those more flattering and often more fashionable hat styles whose brims cast a shadow on the wearer's face, or whose trimmings concealed the profile from one side.

It was to a large extent the example set by Queen Mary which was responsible for the full and active public life now lead by all adult members of the Royal Family, and taken for granted by the rest of the world. She was the first Queen ever to move freely, and almost daily, among the people, and the great change which the new reign of 1910 brought in the royal way of life was, in the opinion of those closest to the throne, at least as much due to her as to her husband. King George V and Queen Mary kept in the closest touch with leaders of all aspects of national life, just as their successors have done. Unlike some of their predecessors, they were always open to suggestions as to how they might better serve their country and its inhabitants.

When, early in their reign, their old friend Cosmo Gordon Lang, who later became Archbishop of Canterbury, was staying with them at Balmoral, he suggested to them that if they were to tour the provinces from time to time they would see for themselves exactly what was going on throughout the country and would also enable hundreds of thousands of their subjects to get to know their new King and Queen much better.

The tour of the northern industrial areas took place in the summer of 1912 and it was a triumphant success. In those days the Royal Family were still known mainly through formal posed portraits; the newsreels and the widely publicized informal photographs had not yet made royalty the familiar personalities they are today. Some of the comments of the crowds were overheard by Queen Mary, while others were reported to her. She was most amused by the often-repeated remark that the King had "got himself a fine upstanding woman for his wife."

The North discovered and approved an unexpected side to Queen Mary's character. Factory managers found her not only interested but well-informed about rates of pay; housewives saw that as soon as she set foot in their houses she knew at once exactly what problems they had to face in the way of steamy kitchens, smoky chimneys and awkward stairs. She was the most practical woman the Royal Family had yet produced.

Throughout her reign as First Lady in the Land, Queen Mary vigorously pursued this policy of seeing as much of Britain and the British people as she could, at work, at play and at home. When her engagements took her, as they often did, among children, she appeared less enchanted than most women are by pretty babies and engaging toddlers. She looked at them with a grave smile, as though she saw the young men or women of the years to come and was anxious that they should be given the chance to

VISIT TO SILVERWOOD COLLIERY, YORKSHIRE
Queen Mary's keen "by-product mind" led her to inspect all that the colliery could produce.

grow into good citizens. She disliked ill-mannered youngsters, but she approved of a certain amount of "toughness" and she admired the signs of an independent spirit. She was delighted, for instance, when a small patient, having been told by the nurses of her forthcoming visit, inquired of her: "Are you the lady wot works in a palace?" Once, when she was given a baby to hold, she pointed out—what had escaped those in charge of it—that it had something wrong with its eyes. She was troubled by the knowledge that a working mother in hospital for the birth of a new baby must always be worrying about what was going on at home, and she was the inspiration behind the addition to a maternity home, which she helped to found, of a wing where the youngest children could be cared for until their mother was strong enough to return home with the new baby. She had a peculiar knack of understanding problems which she herself never had to face, and it was this which made her so different from the kindly but less well informed and less imaginative royal ladies of the past.

She saw to it that her activities, and investigations, were not limited to official tours. Unannounced and often unrecognized, sometimes with a doctor's wife for her guide, she had always made a habit of visiting such districts as the East End of London, demanding to be shown not the latest housing projects and welfare institutions, but the worst slums which could be found. She said little, but was always deeply moved by what she saw. She would return to the royal home to urge others also to go and see for themselves and to pursue with renewed energy some campaign for the betterment of the least privileged of her husband's subjects.

As the wife of a constitutional sovereign she could not interfere with affairs which

ROYAL VISIT TO SOUTH WALES

A pit pony, led by a miner, draws Queen Mary round the Lewis Merthyr Colliery on a trolley.

A FRIEND TO ALL CHILDREN

Queen Mary photographed with boys and girls at a summer home for poor children at Wrotham; the toys were a present from the Queen.

QUEEN MARY VISITS HACKNEY

A familiar friend to the East End, Queen Mary is seen here reading the roll of honour during a wartime visit to Hackney in 1916.

were, ultimately, the responsibility of the Government of the day. But no law of etiquette prevented her from encouraging either private or organized philanthropy which could at least alleviate some of the suffering which she knew to exist. Her personal influence, too, was great and she did much to arouse the social conscience of all those—including the politicians—with whom she came into contact.

Against sweated labour she waged perpetual war. She would inquire, from those who waited upon her for orders for goods supplied to the royal households or for her own use, exactly what wages were paid to their employees and what sort of working hours and conditions prevailed. In some cases the strong suspicion that if she were not satisfied she might arrive in person to investigate resulted in a distinct improvement in factory or workshop. Of any visitor or official who was inclined to paint a rosy picture of social conditions she would gently ask, mentioning a particularly bad slum area, "Have you been into the houses there?" and go on to describe one or two of her own experiences.

When the First World War broke out Queen Mary was quick to realize what it would mean in terms of personal hardship, quite apart from the dangers of active service. The supply of "comforts" through her own Needlework Guild, which recruited more than a million voluntary workers by 1918, and provided nearly four million garments in the first two years of the war, represented only one side of her war work. Although the shortage of manpower was eventually to create employment for all who sought it, the change-over from peace to war left many women unemployed, while others faced for the first time the necessity to become breadwinners. Queen Mary was one of the first people to appreciate that the sudden appearance of a great army of voluntary women workers, although these were inspired by admirably patriotic motives, was a serious menace to the livelihood of other less fortunate women. She therefore initiated the Central Committee on Women's Employment, the preliminary meetings being held in her presence at Buckingham Palace within a few days of the outbreak of war. The Committee later became officially established under Government auspices, but she maintained her link with it by means of the Queen's Fund which she set up to collect money to finance its activities.

This marked a complete departure from the normal charitable and social welfare work in which royalty had previously interested themselves. Although the campaign was non-political, in that it benefited equally women of any, or no, political party, representatives of the Labour Party and of the trade unions played a leading part in its work and consequently came into close contact with Queen Mary at the Palace as well as outside. They found, to their amazement, that the Queen was not merely interested in "charity"; she thoroughly understood the trade-union point of view.

War brought an intensification of another side of Queen Mary's public work; her

QUEEN MARY TOURS NOTTINGHAM AND DERBY
Always interested in workers and their welfare, Queen Mary watches a young employee at a tin works.

interest in hospitals. Every week, and in some weeks almost every day, she visited wards where the wounded were being nursed. It was an exhausting task, since she not only talked to scores of patients in each hospital, but also liked to discuss with doctors and nurses the problems of the moment, with a view to seeing how she and her many friends could best come to their help.

Her household noticed how, back at home in the evenings, Queen Mary would often be "grey with fatigue," her normally lovely complexion having lost all its colour. They alone appreciated quite how much these hospital visits cost her in effort of will. For the Queen, like many exceptionally healthy people, was always greatly affected by the sight of illness. It was not that she ever feared infection; as a young woman she had with characteristic lack of fuss herself taken invalid comforts to a poor cottager shunned by neighbours on account of the highly infectious nature of her disease. But the sight of suffering caused her acute mental and almost physical distress which remained with her long after she had left the sufferer comforted by a sympathetic smile and a cheerful word of greeting.

Sometimes her visits of inspection were almost disconcertingly thorough. No one had, for instance, anticipated that when she visited a vast ammunition factory she would insist on entering the "danger huts" where, so great was the risk of accident, small teams of women worked in isolation in order to minimize the disastrous results of explosion. The necessary rubber overshoes and other safety clothing had to be

QUEEN MARY VISITS THE WOUNDED

The First World War intensified Queen Mary's interest in hospitals, and she cheered many a wounded Serviceman with a kindly smile and friendly word. She is seen (left) with the King on a wartime visit to wounded Indian troops, and (above) at Haslemere in 1918 talking to convalescents.

QUEEN MARY VISITS HOUSING EXHIBITION, 1919

British industry owed much to Queen Mary's support and interest during the difficult years after the
First World War. Her knowledge of housing problems was of great practical help.

hastily procured for her. Visiting workers' canteens she would cause consternation by demanding to see the kitchens and to look inside the store cupboards. Whenever she encountered a problem she had almost always some practical and often simple solution to suggest, which officials had been "too busy" to discover, such as the provision of rough wooden platforms to make it less tiring for short women who had to use sinks and benches designed for tall men. If ever she found avoidable dirt or disorder she had no need to pass comment on it; her reproving glance was sufficient to ensure that something would be done about it as soon as she left.

Armistice Day, 1918, found Queen Mary, a small Union Jack in her hand, standing beside her husband on the balcony of Buckingham Palace, not for one brief appearance but for a total of several hours. Back they came, again and again, until midnight, so that none who came, however late, to join the surging crowds outside should be disappointed.

The end of the war brought Queen Mary no respite from public work; it merely meant that her energies were directed into new channels. She had the gift of seeing national problems in terms of the human suffering which they caused, and it was no exaggeration to say that the widespread unemployment and all that it meant to the families of the unemployed caused her real personal distress. While she was an active supporter of many charitable organizations, she always preached that it was work and not charity which could provide the only lasting solution.

She had always, as a matter of principle, bought goods of British manufacture, and now she took an active part in the encouragement of British industry. She rarely made any purchase without first considering not merely how she could obtain best value for money, but how her custom could be bestowed in order to do most good. She was tireless in visiting trade exhibitions, and she either took her housekeeper with her or first collected "shopping lists" of everything needed in the various Palace departments in order that she could make as many purchases as possible without buying anything which she did not actually need. She always gave permission for goods similar to those which she had chosen to be labelled accordingly, being well aware that the amount of her own purchases was trifling in comparison with those of the many buyers who would order a replica of whatever "Queen Mary had chosen."

There was one aspect of public life which never appealed to Queen Mary personally. She never made speeches. She never broadcast in her life, and on the rare occasions when she spoke "in public" it was only to utter a few simple sentences to a small gathering of people drawn together by a common interest, as when she opened the Mary Macarthur Memorial Home, founded in memory of the great trade-union leader who had become one of her close personal friends.

Queen Mary was no orator, and her own contribution to the life of the nation lay

QUEEN MARY IN SHOREDITCH

Always a friend to children, especially the sick and the poor, Queen Mary is seen here with a small patient in the Caxton Road Hospital during a visit made in 1922.

WIMBLEDON, 1926

A smiling Queen receives Mlle Suzanne Lenglen on the Centre Court. Queen Mary's enthusiasm for tennis is well known and has made her a familiar figure at Wimbledon.

not in speaking but in doing. Her public appearances merely supplemented the great activity which she carried on behind the scenes. Just as in the war no problem had been too vast for her to tackle, so in the peace no contribution which she could make towards national recovery was too small to merit her attention. Thus it was that comparatively few people realized at the time how much the workers of Lancashire, for instance, owed to the Queen who wore cotton dresses when the cotton industry was going through its deep depression, or the Nottingham lace workers owed to the fact that lace curtains appeared at some of the windows of Buckingham Palace at a time when their vogue was declining elsewhere.

Queen Mary's encouragement of the smaller industries, being, as it were, more direct, was more widely known. The custom which she and her many friends brought to the workshops set up to provide employment for disabled ex-servicemen greatly helped to establish these on a sound economic footing. Her strong belief in encouraging those who helped themselves led her, one day when she had a few minutes to spare, to visit a small shop for *objets d'art* which had been opened in the West End by an ex-serviceman. Seeing that the owner was engaged with other customers, and anxious that no trade should be lost through her presence, she indicated that she would look around until he was free. When, after a few minutes, some other clients arrived they saw her at the back of the shop and mistook her for a particularly elegant and dignified saleswoman. The Queen played her part to such perfection that they never discovered their mistake.

Queen Mary always loved paying informal visits and it was on such occasions that the world beyond the Palace gates saw the other side of her majestic personality, the friendly, sympathetic and even homely woman who was known to her intimate friends. One of the few outdoor games which she had ever played herself was lawn tennis and this was also one of the few sports which she really enjoyed watching. Every year she would pay at least one visit to the Wimbledon tournament, and if she could not arrive for the opening of play, she would have a telephone inquiry made to ascertain how her arrival could be timed so as not to interrupt the players. One afternoon, during an exceptionally hot season, since the war, she noticed that a woman spectator, sitting just below her box, was much troubled by the strong sun and was shading her eyes with her hand. Queen Mary leant forward, tapped her on the shoulder and offered her fan as a shade.

On the day that he ascended the throne King George V had written in his diary: "God will help me in my great responsibilities, and darling May will be my comfort as she has always been." After the King's serious illness of 1928 those words were to become more true than they had ever been before. In Queen Mary's unremitting vigilance over the King's health, the duties of private life and public service merged.

In carrying out the loving task of a wife who constantly watches over her husband's welfare she was also preserving the fitful strength of a well-loved sovereign. By her spiritual support, as well as by her practical ministrations, Queen Mary helped to lengthen the King's short lease of life in a way which the royal doctors believed to be little short of miraculous.

As the programme for each of the King's official engagements was drawn up she would scrutinize it to see how it could be adapted to spare him fatigue. When he

WIMBLEDON, 1950

Age has not lessened Queen Mary's interest in her favourite sport—she was eighty-three when this picture was taken. Also in the royal box are (extreme left) *Lord Simon and* (right) *Mr. and Mrs. Attlee.*

TWENTY-FIVE YEARS KING AND QUEEN

With his devoted wife beside him King George V drove to St. Paul's Cathedral in May, 1935, for a Thanksgiving Service to mark the Silver Jubilee of his accession. Few realized how much the nation owed to Queen Mary, without whose care and help the King might never have lived to see his Jubilee.

JUBILEE PROCESSION

London's gaily decorated streets were lined with cheering thousands as the King and Queen drove among them. Only a few months later the widowed Queen Consort became the Queen Mother; but her service to her country has never ceased.

appeared in public she would be at his side, watching for any opportunity which would give him a brief respite to avoid overtaxing his powers. She was the royal doctors' secret ally, and she went about her task so unobtrusively that in 1935 the nation and the Commonwealth were able to celebrate the Silver Jubilee of the reign, little knowing how precarious had been the Sovereign's hold on life for the past seven years, while the King himself was able to carry on his work almost up to his last hours on earth.

When King George V died at Sandringham on 20 January, 1936, Queen Mary's reign as Consort ended as it had begun. Eight days later she stood once again before the open vault in the St. George's Chapel at Windsor Castle and this time she was draped in the veil of widowhood. For almost a year to come she would still be First Lady in the Land, but it was as Queen Mother and no longer Queen Consort that she took part in that ceremony which stands alone in sombre magnificence and solemn splendour: the funeral of a British King.

MARLBOROUGH HOUSE
Queen Mary's permanent and much-loved London home.

QUEEN MARY AND THE
ROYAL HOMES

To understand what Queen Mary has done for the royal homes of Britain one has only to scan the memoirs and letters of the great, written within the past hundred years. Those who have been the Sovereign's guests in recent decades pay tribute to the gracious homeliness of the private rooms, the beauty of the State apartments and the loving artistry with which the royal treasures are displayed therein. They recount the small, thoughtful details of hospitality which betoken a well-ordered household. But in the Victorian era and well into the present century visitors had a different story to tell, for even that kindly host and discerning connoisseur, King Edward VII, was not spared long enough to see the Sovereign's establishments run entirely as he himself would have wished. Being entertained by royalty, always an honour, was only a generation or two ago also an ordeal. The present régime which has made it a pleasure as well as a privilege to visit or stay in one of the royal residences is largely due to the precedents laid down by Queen Mary.

As the Consort of King George V she brought a new influence to the royal way of life. She was by far the best-educated and most cultivated woman the Royal Family had yet known, so that she was both intellectually and artistically better fitted than any of her predecessors to care for the treasures of the royal inheritance. But she was also more "homely," in the best sense of the word, than any of those who had preceded her in the occupation of the Sovereign's homes. Consequently she ran the royal residences with the same personal attention to detail that any good housewife gives to her family home.

The apartments at Kensington Palace and White Lodge, Richmond, where Queen Mary spent her girlhood, had both been small enough for her, as the only daughter of the house, to take an intimate part in their management. She was never called upon to scrub a floor or cook the dinner, but she knew how such things should be done and she also knew the family circumstances of those who did them for her. She also knew how often silver had to be polished and chimneys swept and how housekeeping bills mounted up if they were not carefully watched.

Queen Mary grew up with that same interest in houses that many women have in clothes and most men have in machinery; she could always enjoy herself exploring a new house or in arranging a room. Both as a girl accompanying her parents and as a married woman with her husband she loved staying with friends, and she was familiar with all of the most famous of the fine old country houses of England and with many

Scottish castles as well. Even as Queen, in the days when regular "at home" hours were still generally observed, she liked calling, unannounced, not as royalty but as a friend. Beyond the fact that everyone rose as she entered the drawing-room and again when she took her leave, and instinctively observed the usual etiquette of waiting for her to address them first, there was never any formality about these visits, and Queen Mary joined in many a feminine gossip about the little domestic problems of daily life. She was never above discussing knitting or the perplexities of bringing up children, and she never obtruded her more intellectual interests in circles not well qualified to appreciate them. In one respect Queen Mary belies her regal looks; almost everyone finds her surprisingly "easy to talk to."

As a visitor she has always liked to be shown any possession of special historic or family interest, and she has rarely refused an invitation to be taken round the garden. Sometimes her interest in houses has taken her into the homes of strangers. If she happened to be passing in her car near any house of which she had heard that it possessed some historical association, she would stop and ask her lady-in-waiting to knock at the door and inquire if she might see inside. The occupants, overawed by the unexpected honour, usually protested that they could have wished for at least a few hours' notice so that they might "get ready," but Queen Mary liked to take people as she found them and she always disliked any suggestion of "window-dressing" for a royal visit.

Once, calling in this unexpected way at a house in a South London suburb, she found a small bridge party in progress and chatted happily to the guests, who cherished life-long memories of the day when they set out to play a friendly game of cards and returned home having been presented to a Queen.

Queen Mary has always regarded houses, large or small, not as mere buildings but as homes. When, for instance, she was shown the first maisonettes which formed part of a great local government housing scheme, of which the designers were immensely proud, she at once pointed out that they were very attractive, but had not nearly enough cupboard space. Where, she wanted to know, were the occupants supposed to keep their china or to store their blankets in summer? Later, when post-war council houses were being planned, she was shown scale models first, in time for several of her suggestions to be incorporated into the final design. In the days when the great steamy weekly wash was a distressingly dominating factor in family life she always urged that the "copper" should be installed in an outside wash-house so that the damp should not penetrate into the larder to send the food stores mouldy or into the living-rooms to ruin the paper on the walls. Architects, who had no doubt received much the same advice on dozens of occasions from harassed housewives, listened when it was Queen Mary who reprimanded their lack of common sense.

In her early married days, when she was not the wife but merely the tenant of the Sovereign, she inevitably took her London residence, at least, much as she found it.

WHITE LODGE, RICHMOND

*The girlhood home of Queen Mary. Here she lived with her parents, the Duke and Duchess of Teck,
and here her eldest son was born.*

As Duchess of York she occupied the apartments at St. James's Palace which had
already many family associations for her. She had known them well as the home, until
1889, of her old grandmother, the Duchess of Cambridge, and previously they had
been occupied by her great-uncle, the Duke of Cumberland, who was also King of
Hanover. In honour of the newly-married Duke and Duchess of York this residence
was renamed York House, the title which it still bears today as the home of the Duke
and Duchess of Gloucester.

York House had already been slightly enlarged, by the inclusion of some adjoining
rooms, at the time when preparations were being made for Queen Mary's marriage to
the Duke of Clarence, who was to have made this his first married home, but the
remodelling of the principal rooms was not undertaken until many years later when
they were tenanted by the Duke of Windsor as Prince of Wales.

But even as a new bride Queen Mary could at least arrange the interior to make
a home after her own heart. Although she furnished this largely with wedding presents,
she had some of the furniture specially made to accord with the Georgian style of the
building. There was, for example, a handsome set of side-tables, in the Adam style,

49

AT HOME IN YORK HOUSE

As the newly-married Duke and Duchess of York, Queen Mary and her husband made these apartments at St. James's Palace, renamed in their honour, their first London home.

made for York House and given by Queen Mary, more than half a century later, to her granddaughter, the present Queen, when, as the newly-married Princess Elizabeth, she first set up house at near-by Clarence House.

As Princess of Wales, Queen Mary moved with her husband to Marlborough House, which, with its State rooms and more commodious household accommodation, was second only to Buckingham Palace in its status as a London residence. She rearranged the fine furniture and pictures which she found there, made room for her existing possessions and incorporated into her home many of the handsome presents which she and her husband had received on the Empire tour. But their occupation, recognized from the beginning to be of only a temporary nature, lasted a mere nine years, and Queen Mary's great influence upon Marlborough House belongs therefore rather to those later years when, as Queen Mother, she made it her much-loved and only home.

When the whole Royal Family moved to Scotland each autumn the Prince and Princess of Wales occupied Abergeldie, the unpretentious house on the Balmoral estate, and for those times when the Court was at Windsor Frogmore House was put at their disposal. Queen Mary has always retained a special affection for this modest Georgian house in the Windsor Great Park, for it often enabled her family to enjoy a few days in the country when circumstances did not permit them to be so far from London as

THE GARDENS AT FROGMORE

The delightful and secluded gardens where, during respites from her busy public life, Queen Mary loved to picnic and play with her young family.

Sandringham. Each season, too, she spent a happy week or so there in late summer, alone with her growing family, while her husband was on board the royal yacht at Cowes. His wife, having no great liking for life afloat, welcomed this opportunity for a quiet rest after the busy London season. She played with the children in the secluded, shady grounds, heard their lessons and took them for picnics, read prodigiously and occasionally rummaged in the attics, where she rescued some fine old prints, relegated there by her Victorian predecessors; for this had, long before, been the home of Queen Victoria's mother, the old Duchess of Kent.

There was one small house which, more than any of her other residences, was for thirty years always "home" to Queen Mary. This was York Cottage, on the Sandringham estate, originally the bachelors' annexe, used to accommodate some of the guests invited to the great parties at Sandringham House by King Edward VII, and slightly enlarged in readiness for the wedding of the Duke and Duchess of York in 1893, when it was renamed accordingly.

Here they arrived on the evening of their wedding day to spend their quiet honeymoon. The horses which drew their carriage on that dry July evening raised so much dust that the newly-married couple presented an odd sight, the bride's white going-away dress being nearly black with the dust which had turned the bridegroom's formal black suit to pale grey. Here they took their first meal alone together, and in the days which followed they would sometimes eat out of doors, overlooking the lake.

A few months later Queen Mary's mother visited her daughter at Sandringham and wrote to a friend that this was the "perfection of an ideal cottage; each room is

YORK COTTAGE

The small house which was, for thirty years, "home" to Queen Mary and her family.

SANDRINGHAM HOUSE

The lovely and spacious house which is the well-loved country home of the Royal Family.

charming in its way and everything in perfect taste and most cosy and comfortable." But with the arrival of even one small occupant of the nursery, and with his parents determined to spend at this, their real home, every moment which could be spared from their busy public lives, the cottage proved uncomfortably cramped. Before long the future Queen Mary was making plans for converting it into the home she really wanted, and having the pleasure of inviting her mother to come down again and see the improvements. A new dining-room had been added (thus releasing an extra little sitting-room) with a guest-room above it, and there was a billiard-room for the men, which at least provided somewhere for them to go and talk in the evenings, even if they did not show any particular devotion to the game. Queen Mary, too, was able to have her own little boudoir, next her bedroom, an arrangement which she has always favoured, for it enables her to "get so much done" in those odd moments which might otherwise be wasted. Her rooms, too, were close to the children's nurseries, so that she was able to keep an eye on her family, however busy she might be. Her only lament was, characteristically: "I wish I had one large working-room."

No one—not even Queen Mary—could have made the Cottage one of the stately homes of England. There were never enough rooms and none was ever quite spacious enough for its purpose. Entertaining on any large scale was out of the question, and even when relatives came to stay some of the Household had usually to be temporarily billeted out. York Cottage had no history worth mentioning and from an architectural point of view it lacked distinction. It had, in fact, much in common with the majority

53

BUCKINGHAM PALACE

The premier royal residence, where treasures worth millions of pounds were restored to their original brilliance through the loving and expert care of Queen Mary.

of British homes, in which almost everything depends entirely upon the atmosphere created by its occupants, and of the warm, friendly, lived-in air of "home" there was at least never any shortage. An Archbishop, visiting Queen Mary and her husband and being taken all over the establishment by them, declared afterwards that the experience reminded him of an occurrence so familiar in his yearly visitations—being shown over a new house by a young curate and his house-proud wife.

When in 1910 there were six children in the nursery and schoolroom and their parents became King and Queen, the inadequacy of their accommodation was more than ever apparent. King George V, forced to transact business of State and family affairs alike from the one small ground-floor sitting-room which also served as his study and "audience chamber," once crossly announced that he believed that his staff roosted in the trees at night, as there seemed to be nowhere else for them to sleep. Yet of all the royal residences York Cottage was the only one which Queen Mary was ever to occupy for more than thirty years together, for it remained her one permanent home from the day when she had come to it as a bride in 1893, throughout her life as Princess of Wales and for more than half the years in which she was Queen Consort. When, in 1925, the death of Queen Alexandra left Sandringham House vacant, it was with relief mingled with regret that the family moved into the more spacious quarters of the "Big House." Today York Cottage, scene of so many royal memories, houses a

54

small private museum on part of the ground floor, while the rest of the building is divided into flats for members of the staff of the estate.

With the accession of King George V in 1910, Queen Mary, together with her husband, gave to the nation and the world as Sovereign and Consort that same shining example of serene family life which they had always set throughout their seventeen years of marriage. Their own standard of fidelity and loyalty, of personal integrity and social responsibility, became the standard of the Court, for to their new and larger household they appointed only those men and women whom they knew to possess the same outlook on life as themselves.

The King showed a preference for men who, like him, had served in the Royal Navy, many of them his own former shipmates, but he never made an appointment without consulting his wife. The Queen chose her ladies from those who were already her close friends, and this in itself was a guarantee of their high moral character. But she demanded from them a good deal more than a deservedly unblemished reputation; they had to be intelligent, energetic and above all sympathetic. Thus, even when "home" became the centre of Court life, the same serene, cosy atmosphere of well-ordered and greatly cherished family life was transferred from Marlborough House to the private apartments on the first floor of Buckingham Palace, from modest Frogmore

WINDSOR CASTLE
On the left is St. George's Chapel, and in the background the Round Tower.

to the Sovereign's wing overlooking the East Terrace of ancient Windsor Castle, and from little Abergeldie to the more imposing turreted residence of Balmoral Castle. Meals were still family occasions; indeed, the Queen and her husband and children more often sat down to table alone now that there was ample separate accommodation for their household.

Small changes betokened the more domestic character of the new reign. At Windsor Castle, for instance, guests found that when the men had finished their port after dinner they joined the womenfolk in one of the drawing-rooms. King George and Queen Mary liked to spend these leisure hours in each other's company, and consequently the guests were no longer segregated according to sex as they had been in former days. The royal host and hostess would take their seats—which meant that the rest of the company were not condemned to spend the evening standing up. This relaxation of etiquette was doubly welcomed. It not only disposed of a certain amount of formality; it was also less tiring. It was a practical gesture from a Queen who herself spent many hours of every day on her feet, towards household and guests whose presence in the royal circle denoted that they, too, were no Society idlers.

From the beginning of the new reign Queen Mary began to devote herself to an ambitious work which, in the lasting quality of its value, perhaps deserves to rank above all her many other achievements. This was the complete reorganization of the major royal homes. No one had ever attempted such a task before, for no one had been equal to it. No one has ever undertaken it since, for it has never again been necessary.

King George V was well content to leave the management of his homes to his wife, recognizing in her not only housewifely qualities but artistic talent far beyond his own. He was immensely proud of the great collection of treasures which were his inheritance, but always when he was displaying them to his guests he would say: "But if you are interested my wife will tell you the exact details," or, if she were near-by, he would call in his deep, booming voice: "May, will you come and tell us all about this?"

Queen Mary felt the same responsibility for every one of her thousands of rooms and hundreds of servants that every good householder feels for the most modest establishment and the smallest domestic staff. No longer were the State rooms to be regarded as detached portions of Palace or Castle whose supervision rested largely with officials responsible for the conduct of Court ceremonial. No longer were kitchens and staff quarters to remain unknown realms into which royalty never ventured to penetrate. Queen Mary was determined that nothing should go on in any royal household which a house-proud British woman would not tolerate in her own establishment. Consequently she made it her business, as for the first time in the new reign the Court moved round in its traditional annual migration from London to Windsor, to Scotland and to Sandringham, to tour every one of the thousands of rooms which for the next quarter of a century were to be in her charge. Queen Mary was certainly the first

BALMORAL CASTLE

The snow-covered castle and grounds, with the imposing Culardoch in the background.

member of the Royal Family who had ever undertaken such a task, involving, from first to last, literally several miles of walking, up and down innumerable stairways, back and fro along endless corridors, in and out of doorways. Indeed, it is doubtful if any one person had ever before inspected every single room, passage and cupboard in every one of the royal homes.

At Buckingham Palace the story is told of how Queen Mary had once got lost as a result of setting out unescorted to investigate some obscure back stair, and of her continuing her voyage of exploration until she finally emerged into a familiar region. At Windsor it was learnt that household officials had tried hard to dissuade her from descending into the store rooms, assuring her that even they had never dared venture into what was traditionally the province of very senior members of the royal staff. At first not everyone approved of a royal mistress who took her responsibilities quite so wholeheartedly. The mere knowledge that at any moment her regal figure might appear round the bend of the corridor set a new standard in cleanliness, orderliness and economy. But soon the staff began to welcome this personal attention, for it became evident that, of the funds available for maintenance and improvement of the royal homes, a larger share than ever before was to be devoted to kitchens and staff quarters.

At Buckingham Palace, where the King and Queen and consequently the majority of their indoor staff spent most of the year, the kitchens were entirely remodelled. More windows were introduced and they were all made to open so as to admit air as well as light. Modern gas cookers were installed, the hot-water supply was improved, better sinks were fitted, both downstairs and on the upper floors, for the benefit of housemaids. Cupboards were made dust- and damp-proof. Sitting-rooms were allocated to each small group of staff and the Queen saw that these were attractively and comfortably furnished, and she herself chose pretty curtains for them and selected suitable pictures for the walls.

Had every Queen loved her homes and their precious possessions as Queen Mary did, the royal residences would have been treasure-houses of untold wealth and unrivalled beauty. As it was, despite the neglect of generations, the contents of Buckingham Palace alone were valued at some four million pounds (their worth today must be more than twice this amount). Much that was beautiful in the legacy of the past was hidden beneath a covering of actual and also metaphorical dust. Queen Mary found experts already engaged upon the task of sorting the dross from the gold, of cataloguing the major works of art and restoring many of these after the ravages of years. King Edward VII had at least appreciated the richness of his inheritance, but this had been his for too few years for the task of putting it into order to be more than well begun.

Queen Mary determined that the royal possessions should not merely be catalogued; she was anxious to record the exact history of every item—and there were many thousands of these—which had any claim to artistic or intrinsic worth or to historical or family interest. Much of the actual research was, necessarily, entrusted to others, but the work was undertaken under the constant supervision of her immensely orderly and highly cultivated mind. The expert members of the household, such as the Royal Librarian at Windsor and the Keeper of the King's Pictures, were given a status which their Victorian predecessors had never known. They were in close personal touch with the Queen, who eagerly welcomed each little scrap of information they could unearth, so that, inspired by her zeal, they recruited the help of many of their erudite friends in recovering the lost history of a vase or picture, or maybe a suite of furniture.

A typical incident concerned a handsome but unidentified dinner service kept at Windsor Castle. Queen Mary, reading a volume of eighteenth-century memoirs, discovered that a service of which she knew nothing had been presented to George III by the King of Sicily. Could these two sets of china be in fact one and the same? Months later the question was answered. Records in the British Museum described George III's gift in such detail that it was easily identified with the dinner service at Windsor, and they also gave the whole history of the china.

The archives at Windsor Castle were searched for old inventories, ledgers and bills, and many objects whose histories were long forgotten were thus able to be identified. Sometimes Queen Mary herself came across a description or picture of some item which had apparently become lost—she discovered in this way that several single articles were in fact survivors of a pair or set, and then the hunt began for the missing pieces. Inevitably there were failures; no doubt fire, theft, the rubbish dump and the indiscriminate generosity of earlier sovereigns accounted for these. But the successes were astonishingly numerous, and many of them were due to Queen Mary's remarkable memory. Her sharp eyes would detect a chair which was almost, but not quite, identical with its fellows, and she would remember where she had seen others which were an exact match, often in quite a different residence. Investigating the contents of a store, she would recognize some object which must have once "belonged" with some other piece which she had possibly not set eyes upon for months. A whole set of little china models, dating from the time of George III, was once collected together in this way. For decades only one of the great throne-like chairs, shown in pictures of the Regent's demolished Palace of Carlton House, had stood in the throne room of Buckingham Palace. Now, as for years past, one chair stands on either side of the dais; Queen Mary found the other one of the pair when touring the apartments at Kensington Palace.

She possesses that strange gift of photographic memory which always enabled her

THE THRONE ROOM AT BUCKINGHAM PALACE

On either side of the throne dais stand the great throne-like chairs from the old Palace of Carlton House. For decades only one stood there—Queen Mary found the other.

to recall exactly where she had seen any particular object. One day she went into a room where, she declared, years before she had been shown a chest full of old silks and tapestries. But there was no chest to be seen and although she caused inquiries to be made no trace of it could be found. It seemed as though, for once, her memory had betrayed her. Then, at last, the missing piece of furniture was discovered—it had been moved from Windsor to London—and the contents were just as she had described them.

Every fact concerning the furniture or works of art was recorded as soon as it was discovered, and thus much fascinating information which might have been lost for ever has been preserved for posterity. Queen Mary herself entered up many of the "histories" in small, bound volumes, just as she has always recorded everything that she knows about her personal possessions. Whenever anything was temporarily relegated to store she had it carefully labelled. Where practicable she wrote brief details on small cards which were inserted in slots hidden away out of sight.

Every royal residence had its capacious store rooms and at Windsor Castle there were whole towers which had been used for storage for a hundred years and more. Queen Mary had these cleared out and herself presided over the final process of sorting, so that what might have been merely a glorified and long overdue spring-cleaning turned into an exciting treasure hunt. Much expert restoration was required. A damaged vase would tell its own little story of the carelessness of some mid-Victorian housemaid or footman who had hastily stowed away the incriminating evidence in the well-justified hope that it would never be missed among the mountains of nineteenth-century bric-à-brac. Sometimes a charming little statue emerged, banished perhaps to make room for one of the many family sculptures commissioned by Queen Victoria, who liked to be able to sit and survey her many relatives in marble when they could not be present in person.

Now and then Queen Mary, in a capacious borrowed apron or overall, would call for good homely soap and water so that she could at once investigate what lay beneath the dust of decades. As the funds available for the upkeep of the royal residences permitted, the apartments were redecorated, a room or a suite at a time, and when the day came to reinstate them she drew upon this great store of rediscovered treasure. The many choice examples of Wedgwood china which came to light gave her the idea of creating a "Wedgwood Room" at Windsor Castle, where she also gathered into the Ministerial suite many fascinating souvenirs of the great statesmen of the past. At Buckingham Palace she made her famous Chinese Chippendale Room which became one of her favourite private sitting-rooms. From the legacy of the Prince Regent's collecting days she created Regency Rooms and Oriental Rooms.

Antique Chinese panels were brought out to cover the walls of the celebrated Balcony Room, and when the furniture of the Green Drawing-room required re-uphol-stering a roll of silk almost contemporary with the chairs and settees themselves was found to yield sufficient material for the purpose. The large sums of money thus saved enabled Queen Mary to complete each room to her satisfaction. She enlisted the help of art experts and antique dealers, so that when the contents of some fine old house due for demolition were put up for sale chandeliers or chimney pieces were bought on her behalf.

Nothing was ever wasted and all manner of ingenious devices were employed, such as many a good housewife has to resort to in order to stretch a limited budget. When the colour scheme of the Palace Picture Gallery was changed from crimson to green, in order to provide a more harmonious background for some of the finest canvases in the King's Collection, the plain strip carpet was not replaced, but merely dyed to Queen Mary's exact specifications.

Each room was photographed from various angles so that when the periodic cleaning was undertaken the contents could be restored to their exact position. Although each new reign brings changes in the private apartments, where the present Queen has introduced some of her own furniture just as her parents did fifteen years ago, the State rooms change little. The handiwork of Queen Mary is everywhere to be seen, although only by those who know where to look for it. The State suites now reflect not the taste of one generation but the history of a whole dynasty, in which the reign of King George V is accorded only its due share, manifested in such embellishments as, for

THE PALACE PICTURE GALLERY

Redecorated and reorganized by Queen Mary to form a fitting background for the Sovereign's collection.

instance, the draperies of the throne dais in the Buckingham Palace ballroom, which were made from the Imperial Shamiana beneath which King George and Queen Mary sat enthroned at the Delhi Coronation Durbar in 1911.

One other Palace still remained—as it does to this day—technically "within the personal occupation of the Sovereign." This was Edinburgh's Palace of Holyroodhouse, the only official royal residence in Scotland. As the Court had never regularly resided there Queen Mary was less well acquainted with Holyroodhouse than with other royal homes, but she had retained, from her first visit when barely into her teens, vivid memories and a great affection for this fine old Palace so closely associated with that other Queen Mary, surnamed of the Scots. The Palace had been so neglected during the nineteenth century (Queen Victoria disliking it because, it was asserted, she believed it to be haunted) that, when King Edward VII had decided to hold there the first Scottish Court for generations, the drains were found to be out of order and he and his Queen had to reside elsewhere.

Ever since Queen Mary first took the Palace under her care Courts have, in normal times, been held there about every third year in addition to other functions, such as garden parties, while the private apartments are kept in a sufficient state of readiness for royalty to reside there for a few days from time to time.

The State rooms, partially reinstated in the Edwardian reign, became year by year

THE BALLROOM AT BUCKINGHAM PALACE

The draperies over the throne dais were made from the Imperial Shamiana beneath which King George and Queen Mary sat enthroned at the Delhi Coronation Durbar of 1911.

THE PALACE OF HOLYROODHOUSE, EDINBURGH

Restored by Queen Mary as a royal residence and centre for the Court when in Scotland.

more beautiful as Queen Mary's plan for their embellishment matured. A new ceiling was bestowed upon the throne room; in Queen Victoria's breakfast room (used when she broke her long railway journey to and from Balmoral) strip lighting has been introduced to illumine the tapestry-hung walls and, although the furniture associated with Prince Albert was still kept in the Consort's room, Queen Mary had new chair panels specially embroidered at the Edinburgh School of Needlework. Women of the great old Scottish families, heartened at seeing their "own" Palace so restored to royal favour, combined to embroider seats for twenty-four Queen Anne chairs in the morning drawing-room, each tapestry being stitched by two noble needlewomen, while Queen Mary herself worked a stool cover.

At Holyroodhouse, as at the English royal residences, visitors seldom progress far without being shown some handsome addition to the furniture "given" by Queen Mary, which explains why, now that she has retired to Marlborough House with her personal treasures, the Castle and Palace rooms remain as she left them, although two Kings have come and gone and once again the royal homes house a "Queen's Collection."

With her major task accomplished, Queen Mary turned her attention to those royal residences of long ago, St. James's Palace, Hampton Court and especially her own girlhood home of Kensington Palace. Here some rooms which she and her parents and family had once occupied formed part of the State apartments open to the public, and

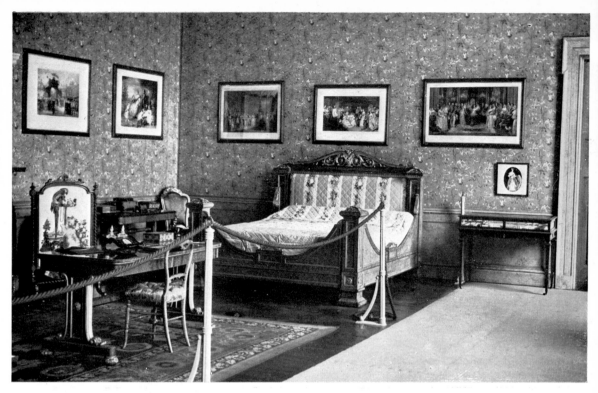

Above: *Queen Victoria's bedroom in Kensington Palace, where Queen Mary herself was born.*
Below: *Queen Victoria's nursery, containing some of her childhood toys which she bequeathed to Queen Mary, who restored them to their rightful place. The piano is one which Prince Albert played.*

KENSINGTON PALACE

The birthplace of Queen Mary, and her family's London home during her childhood.

under her guidance these were restored to something approximating to their mid-nineteenth-century appearance. Among these rooms was that in which she herself was born and which, before her day, the future Queen Victoria and her mother had shared as a bedroom. Queen Mary was delighted when it was discovered that the makers of the quaint little rosebud-pattern wallpaper still possessed the original blocks, so that the room could be redecorated without destroying its period character.

Much of the furniture had been dispersed, but Queen Mary saw that it was replaced with pieces similar to those which it had contained in her childhood days—there is still an old-fashioned washstand, with a small jug and basin brought from Windsor Castle. To her old nursery Queen Mary restored some of the dolls and mechanical playthings which Queen Victoria had left to her—toys with which the great Queen and Empress had once played in that same room. The dainty walnut desk, gift of her mother, at which Queen Mary did her early lessons, is now, thanks to her, back in its old place. To complete the picture, there are many little odds and ends lent from her vast collection of royal souvenirs, such as the programme of one of the first State concerts which she attended at Buckingham Palace and the menu of a magnificent banquet held there in her youth. Thus Kensington and the other royal homes of former days remain, like those in which her granddaughter and her great-grandchildren live today, to bear testimony to Queen Mary's love and understanding of her family's great heritage of beautiful and historic things.

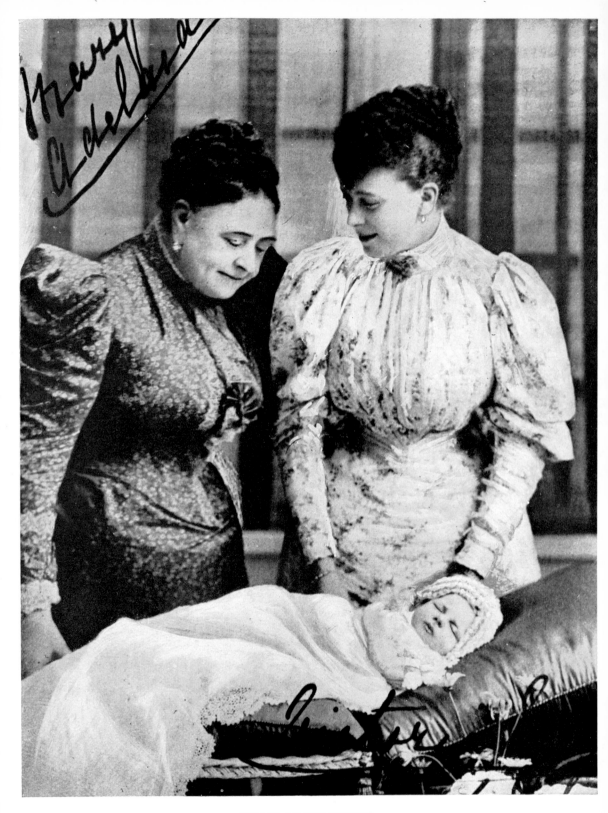

THREE GENERATIONS

An autographed portrait of Queen Mary, then Duchess of York, with her mother, the Duchess of Teck, and her first son, Prince Edward, now the Duke of Windsor.

WIFE, MOTHER AND
GRANDMOTHER

The crown of a British Queen Consort is the symbol of one of the most exacting offices in the modern world. While the rest of her regalia has been handed down from Stuart days, a new crown has been created for the wife of each Sovereign since the seventeenth century, a token—so the lover of signs and portents might say—that the wearer must fashion out her own place in the life of her husband's realm. The Constitution, while acknowledging her status, lays down few specific functions for her to fulfil, although the Church, recognizing that something beyond devotion to wifely duty is demanded of the woman who is wedded not only to her husband but also to his people, provides the Queen Consort with a separate Coronation ritual, to be performed even in the event of her marrying a King already crowned.

History has all too much to tell of wives who, far from sharing the burden of the Sovereign's crown, added yet further to its weight, and the "good" Queens of the past were often deemed so largely because they were virtuous as well as beautiful and sufficiently self-effacing to confine themselves to the comparatively passive role of domesticity and works of charity. The modern conception of the Queen Consort, as a woman actively sharing in her husband's public life (without encroaching upon his constitutional duties) and at the same time undertaking a full public life of her own, is almost entirely due to Queen Mary's example.

Few women had ever been by nature so well fitted to be the wife of a British Sovereign; no one had ever striven so earnestly and so successfully to fit herself yet better for such a life of dual service to family and nation.

Today, when almost sixty years have passed since their wedding, the world sees in the union of King George and Queen Mary a standard of perfection by which all other marriages might well be judged. But if this was, from its beginning, a love match, then the Providence which watches over princes granted to the future King George V the happy dispensation of choosing for his bride the one woman whom those best qualified to judge would have chosen for him. The era of the "arranged" betrothal was by no means over, and one spring day in 1893 the Prime Minister, the veteran Mr. Gladstone, waited on Queen Victoria to request, on behalf of the Government and the nation which it represented, that she would use her influence to bring about the marriage of the ultimate heir to the throne with Princess May of Teck. But the Queen needed no such urging; both sides of the family (admittedly with one or two notable exceptions, who soon, however, discovered their misgivings to be ill-founded) were ready to welcome the engagement and, indeed, generally believed that they would not have long to wait for news of it. On 3 May "Georgie," as she always called the Prince, asked his grandmother's consent by telegram. After giving this "gladly," Queen Victoria confided to her journal: "I have so much wished for this engagement that it gives me the greatest satisfaction." Four years later, when time and experience had confirmed the wisdom of her judgment, she was to exclaim: "Thank God Georgie has got such an excellent, useful and good wife."

A little more than a week after the wedding the bridegroom was telling one of his oldest friends: "I am intensely happy; far happier than I ever thought I could be with anyone." This was no short-lived illusion, seen through the rose-tinted spectacles of honeymoon days. The same sentiment re-echoes again and again in his journal and letters throughout the next forty years and more. Writing home to his mother, Queen Alexandra, during the Empire tour of 1901, the Duke of Cornwall and York, as he was then known, reported: "Darling May is the greatest possible help to me and works very hard. I don't think I could have done all this without her. Everyone admires her very much, which is very pleasing to me. I hope you are as proud of your daughter-in-law as I am of my wife." In recording any great event, as in chronicling the smaller episodes of family life, he almost invariably alluded to his "darling May," and referred in almost identical terms (being a man of few and simple words) to the never-failing source of comfort and strength which he found in her presence beside him.

Even today it is by no means an easy task for a woman to be a good wife and mother and still pursue an active and busy life whose duties necessarily often take her into the outside world beyond the home. Half a century ago, with the emancipation of women still a goal on the far horizon, such an ambition would have been regarded as a crime and its achievement as an impossibility. Yet, looking back over the years, who can point to a woman who has enjoyed either a more active "career" or a fuller family life than Queen Mary?

The Victorian world who saw her married and the Edwardians who watched her children growing up might well, could they have seen into the future, have condemned a woman who planned to combine so many outside interests with those of husband and home and sons and daughter. Paradoxically, the one great example before her was that of Queen Victoria herself, who had personally supervised the minutest details of the upbringing of her nine children throughout the years when she reigned as the most powerful Sovereign in Europe.

Queen Mary so contrived her life that few people realized how much she was accomplishing. A great deal of her work passed under the guise of that social life and spasmodic charitable activity which was an accepted part of the duty of the wife of a public man. Those visitors whom her husband chose to introduce into the privacy of his home found her always there. But the distinguished guests were never permitted to

THE ROYAL COUPLE

An early picture of King George V and Queen Mary.

while away the hours with conventional small talk. Queen Mary would profit by their visits to discover exactly what problems confronted those who worked and moved in spheres other than her own, and often put forward her own solutions so tactfully that when these suggestions came to be adopted, as they so often were, it was seldom realized that they had originally come from her.

It was one of the greatest tributes to Queen Mary's devotion as a wife that only those closest to the throne could ever say which of the royal decisions, which projects emanating from Buckingham Palace, which features, in short, of the royal way of life, owed their inspiration to her and which to her husband. Many of the changes technically initiated by King George V were attributed, by those best qualified to judge, to the advice of his wife. On the other hand, Queen Mary was content to be credited with responsibility for many little matters which were, in fact, entirely due to her meticulous observance of her husband's wishes. Even her long dresses, which caused so much comment in the days when other women's skirts grew shorter every year, owed their defiance of fashion to the King's disapproval of a vogue which affronted his Victorian sense of propriety. His wife, while disliking the ugly ultra-short skirts which prevailed for a brief while in the 1920's, occasionally confessed that she was not sorry to see women more hygienically and practically clad than they had been in the days of her youth. One of her "ladies," coming into waiting at Balmoral, appeared one evening in a trailing "picture gown" on which King George V commented with much approval. Queen Mary, however, was less enthusiastic. "Oh, my dear," she sighed to her lady-in-waiting afterwards, "it is a very charming dress, but I had only just got the King to agree to my wearing my skirts another inch above the ground."

Certainly no woman ever studied her husband's comfort, and even his occasionally capricious whims, more zealously than did Queen Mary. "She is," wrote a visitor to her early married home, "gentle and homely in a rather stately way," and this—one instinctively feels—was exactly what her husband wished his wife to be. Queen Mary spent more than forty years of her life ministering to a man who loved cosiness as much as he revered ceremony, who kept a frock-coat hanging in his study so that he might work in the comfort of an old jacket and yet be always ready to grant an audience dressed as, in his opinion, a Sovereign should be dressed.

At Sandringham, when he came in from shooting, Queen Mary would be waiting, and, no matter how many guests were assembled in the anticipation of a formal afternoon tea, her very presence was a guarantee that he would have his boiled egg cooked for exactly the right number of seconds to set it just as he liked it. A woman, unacquainted with royal circles, who visited King George and Queen Mary during one of the King's periods of convalescence at the seaside, was delighted to find the Queen presiding over a tea-table on which reposed that familiar sight in every British home, a jar of home-made jam still wearing, as she described it, "its little paper hat."

Within the life of the family Queen Mary saw to it that "Papa" took pride of

QUEEN CONSORT AND QUEEN MOTHER

Queen Mary photographed with Queen Alexandra when they attended a Red Cross exhibition in 1918.

A KING'S FUNERAL

*The young Prince of Wales and his brother, Prince Albert, both destined in turn to reign as King,
walked in the procession at the funeral of King Edward VII.*

place. Thus it was that one of the few great family and State occasions which she has
missed in the whole of her long adult life was the funeral of Queen Victoria. On the
winter day when the great Queen made her last journey to Windsor her grandson,
the new Duke of Cornwall and York, was ill at Sandringham with measles and his wife
stayed to nurse him while their eldest children attended the ceremony without her.
Yet no one could have more deeply desired to pay a last tribute to the old Queen whom
she so loved and venerated, for when a day or two later the invalid was well enough
to be left, and the Duchess of Cornwall and York attended the second ceremony at the
Mausoleum at Frogmore, of all the illustrious company present the future Queen Mary
and one of Queen Victoria's youngest grandsons alone were seen to weep.

Queen Mary was the first British royal mother who deliberately set out to give
her children an upbringing which differed as little as possible from that of other boys
and girls who, like them, were born into a cultured and comfortable home. Not one of
her children was born in any of the major royal residences, and this is particularly
significant, for there were many precedents—and some of these recent—for royal
mothers-to-be hastening for the happy event to stay beneath the roof of some palace

or castle which they did not normally inhabit. For the arrival of the future King Edward VIII his mother retired to the comparative obscurity of her parents' home at White Lodge, Richmond. The second son, destined to reign as King George VI, was, like his sister and all his younger brothers, born at York Cottage, Sandringham. Until their schoolroom days were over visits to London were kept to a minimum, and as many months as possible of every year were spent in the country where life was more free and easy and the local population took royalty for granted, so that the consciousness of their royal rank rarely obtruded itself into their young minds.

Royalty are, by tradition, always credited in official bulletins with having given birth to a Prince or a Princess, and never to a mere son or daughter. Was not the great Duke of Wellington rebuked when to his eager question "Is it a boy?" the royal nurse, Mrs. Lilly, replied: "Your Grace, it is a Prince!" But each new addition to the York (later the Wales) household was welcomed with as much homely parental pride as ever greeted a new-born subject.

Many pages of the family albums were soon dedicated to the photographic records of the small Princes and their only sister. In addition their mother opened a book for each child wherein she entered such fascinating statistics as its weight at birth, the date of its first tooth and many other such illuminating facts about its juvenile progress through life. In true Victorian tradition a lock of hair, snipped off on the occasion of the first hair-cut, was incorporated into each "file."

Popular imagination has tended to portray King George V as a stern Victorian

THE YOUNG PRINCES IN PUBLIC

The young princes at a Royal Garden Party with their mother and Queen Alexandra.

REVIEW OF VETERANS AT PORTSMOUTH, 1911
The young Duke of York accompanied his parents on this naval occasion.

parent, and no doubt the fathers of half a century ago did wield their authority with a heavier hand than do their present-day successors. But, as Duke of York, his friends found him "very much the family man" and he was assiduous in his attendance at the evening ceremony of the baby's bath. He showed a sailor's efficiency in coping with this new undertaking and was delighted when he was promoted from the status of an admiring onlooker to that of an executive officer. Recounting one of these early experiences to one of the Queen's ladies he boasted: "I made a very good lap." A family tradition was thus established, for since that time all our royal mothers and fathers have interested themselves in the delicate but entertaining task of bathing baby. Visiting Clarence House as a great-grandmother, Queen Mary was once invited by the small Prince Charles to visit him in his bath, and although pressure of other engagements made it necessary for her to decline she sent up a message indicating that a similar invitation would be welcome some other time.

Queen Mary, with her own happy memories of her childhood companionship with her father, saw to it that her children, too, enjoyed the company of "Papa" whenever possible. He, consequently, felt almost as much as his wife the long absences from the family necessitated by the Empire tour and other visits abroad. When, during their tour of Canada in 1901, a local woman resident mistook the Duke of Cornwall and York for one of his equerries and plied him with questions about the Duchess, he obligingly answered these without revealing his identity. But when his questioner finally expressed the universal sympathy which the Canadians felt for a mother thus parted from her young family, the royal visitor exclaimed: "And what about me—they're my children, too, you know."

In a household thus subject to enforced separations, great store was set by all those occasions which help to bring a family together and strengthen the bonds of home life. Parents' as well as children's birthdays were always observed with due ceremony, and the young people planned their presents long in advance and valiantly strove to keep these as surprises. On Mamma's or Papa's birthday, recitations, sometimes in French and always carefully rehearsed, were delivered, each child also handing over a neatly written copy of the text. Queen Mary liked to keep these performances as private as possible, suspecting, with her unfailing common sense, that what might well delight a fond parent might prove less entertaining to a larger audience. Their father took a great interest in these recitations, which marked his children's progress from year to year. On 26 May, 1906, "darling May's 39th birthday," he wrote that the children had all recited their poems, adding: "David [now the Duke of Windsor, then in his twelfth year] did it quite extraordinarily well. He said Wolsey's Farewell (Shakespeare) without a mistake."

Except for birthdays and, of course, Christmas, which was always kept up in the traditional way at Sandringham, Queen Mary did not greatly approve of parties for her youngsters. Friends who invited one or other of the children to tea would often receive

75

a courteous little note from their mother explaining that she was sorry but their lessons must not be interrupted.

To Queen Mary "education" in its widest sense was always one of life's most important duties. With her it was a continuous process. She was already the mother of several children when the late Lord Esher, scholar, statesman and confidential adviser to three generations of the Royal Family, remarked after a long conversation with her: "She is educating herself carefully and will one day be a woman of much importance," a comment eloquent in its understatement. In later years Queen Mary often confessed that as a young woman she had been shocked to realize how "uneducated" she herself was—a state of affairs which she at once set out to remedy. But how much greater, if less openly expressed, must have been her horror at the lack of "education" evinced by most of her royal relatives. She was always desperately anxious that her children should be given the best possible preparation for the life which lay ahead of them, and many people believed that she would, had the choice rested entirely with her, have been glad to see her sons benefit from a normal public-school régime. Her brother had been the first member of the Royal Family to be entered at Eton, but etiquette still required the elder sons of the heir to the throne to be, like his daughter, educated at home until the time came for them to embark upon training for one of the services.

In each of her homes, until the advent of the First World War, Queen Mary established a schoolroom and a school curriculum in whose ordering she herself played a prominent part. There was a tutor for the boys and a governess for Princess Mary, and advice was often sought in addition from that highly-cultivated and well-informed Madame Bricka who had guided their mother's own early search for knowledge.

Anxious that her children should, like her, grow up with an easy command of languages, she engaged German nannies so that one foreign tongue at least was acquired with comparative ease in nursery days. French also figured largely in the curriculum and on certain days had to be spoken throughout meals. The school time-table was rigidly observed—two hours' work after breakfast, a thirty-minute break and then another hour of lessons before lunch. The afternoon was occupied by games and exercise, followed by more study until tea.

To supplement the early instruction in simple prayers and Bible stories which they learnt from their mother, and their regular attendance at church, the royal children all had Scripture lessons from one of the clergy attached to the King's Household. To offset the isolation of the royal schoolroom the children were encouraged to play with companions of their own age, and thus the village football teams at Sandringham were captained by two future Kings, while their sister joined a number of young friends in "gym" and dancing classes.

Visitors to York Cottage were often surprised by the exuberance and unself-consciousness of their host's young family. "All the children tumbled about the floor with a rocking-horse and toys while we had our coffee," commented a family friend,

ROYAL FAMILY GROUP

Queen Mary with three of her growing family—the Prince of Wales, Prince Albert and Princess Mary.

after a visit in 1908, when the ages of the six youngsters ranged from three to fourteen. The children joined their parents at meals at an age when many of their contemporaries were still relegated to the nursery table. When they were at the schoolroom stage their mother liked them to be present even when there were strangers invited, and she arranged the seating so that the elder children sat next to one of the visitors and so had to join in the conversation and share the parents' responsibility for hospitality.

After tea their mother almost invariably gathered the children round her in her boudoir, where she read aloud to them, thus combining her own before-dinner rest with a quiet children's hour until their early bedtime arrived. She also taught the boys as well as their sister various kinds of needlework. Although these might be regarded as unusual accomplishments for men, all her sons returned to these childhood hobbies for relaxation or to while away hours of enforced idleness in adult life. The Duke of Windsor crocheted and knitted both during a period of convalescence and in spells of inactivity during his war service; the late Duke of Kent knitted mufflers while at sea, and the late King George VI, like his younger brother, the Duke of Gloucester, some-

77

times found embroidering such articles as chair seats a soothing form of occupation.

None of the royal homes, not even Buckingham Palace, could have been described as luxurious as far as the family living quarters were concerned, while the smaller residences provided an austere and almost spartan background owing to their lack of modern amenities. The royal children were singularly unspoiled; "treats" of any kind were rare and late nights even rarer, while their mother strictly regulated their pocket money, so that any indulgence in the way of extra sweets depended upon a timely tip from an open-handed grandfather or generous guest.

Across the even progress of this extremely simple family life there swept from time to time the excitement, the bustle and the colour of a State occasion. Queen Mary liked her children, from an early age, to take part in any great national celebration which they could suitably attend, so that the people might get to know them, at least by sight, while they themselves might gradually become accustomed to the kind of life which lay ahead of them. They made their first "balcony appearances" with other members of the Royal Family when little more than toddlers, while at the funeral of

THE ROYAL FAMILY IN WARTIME

Silver Wedding group taken in July, 1918. Left to right: *Prince Albert, Prince George, Queen Mary, Prince Henry, King George and Princess Mary.*

FAMILY GATHERING AT BALMORAL, 1923
Queen Mary with the Duke and Duchess of York and (left) the late Duke of Kent.

King Edward VII the two young sons of the new Sovereign, who were both destined in turn to occupy the throne, walked in the procession. All the children attended their father's and mother's Coronation, with the exception of the youngest, Prince John. This little Prince was in any case too small to accompany the rest of the family on these early State appearances and he was rarely seen in public owing to the delicate health which lasted until his death, at the age of thirteen, in 1919, although he usually watched the great processions from the windows of Buckingham Palace.

By ensuring that her children thus participated in great national events, Queen Mary did much to strengthen the ties which bound them to their father's people, for in adult life they could thus look back and feel that they had from their earliest years fully shared in the joys and sorrows of the nation. There were other ways, too, in which their mother handed on to them her own love and understanding of the royal traditions. "I talked to the children about the dear Queen," she wrote when Queen Victoria died, "so that they may never forget their great-grandmother."

Although Queen Mary's personal recollections were limited to the later decades of the great Queen's life, she could also bring her children into close contact with one whose vivid and accurate memory not only spanned the whole of Queen Victoria's

THE FIRST GRANDCHILD

In 1923 Queen Mary became a grandmother for the first time. She holds in her arms the Princess Royal's first son, now the Earl of Harewood, whose own small son is her third great-grandchild.

reign but stretched back into the days of George IV. This was her aunt, her mother's sister, the Grand Duchess of Mecklenberg-Strelitz, known to all the family as "Aunt Augusta." This remarkable woman, who died at the age of ninety-four in 1916, had not only attended the Coronations of Queen Victoria and William IV, but also remembered the day when she was patted on the head by their predecessor, George IV. Although she had married into a German ducal family she never abandoned her claim to be known as a Princess of Great Britain, and she remained a regular visitor to her English relatives until well into the reign of King George V and Queen Mary, whose Coronation, like that of King Edward VII, she attended.

Queen Mary instilled into her children a great respect for all their older relatives, whom the boys would greet with a bow while their sister dropped a curtsey. In later life, when the pressure of public engagements left little leisure for personal affairs, the younger generation were always attentive to their great-aunts and elderly cousins. They divided this responsibility among themselves—the late Duke of Kent, for instance, visited his great-aunt, Princess Louise, at Kensington Palace almost every Friday afternoon until her death in 1939—so that those relatives who were forced into semi-retirement by reason of advancing years were always able to retain close ties with the Sovereign's family.

The same spirit of family unity was seen when Queen Mary's children grew up

ROYAL CHRISTENING IN WARTIME

Queen Mary attends the christening in 1942 of the Duke of Kent's third child, not long before the Duke's tragic death. Four royal exiles stand with the late King and the Duke—Prince Bernhard of the Netherlands, King Haakon of Norway, King George of the Hellenes and Crown Prince Olav of Norway.

and married. Their mother, herself the granddaughter of a morganatic marriage, rejoiced as one by one her children sought their father's permission to marry the partner of their choice. While each young household looked to King George V as the head of the family, it was to Queen Mary that they turned for advice on all the more domestic and personal problems which arose as the years went by.

In February, 1923, Queen Mary entered upon a new phase of her life, for she became a grandmother for the first time. Her family of grandchildren was well balanced: first came the Princess Royal's two sons, the present Earl of Harewood and his brother Gerald, born eighteen months later; then there were two little girls, the present Queen and her sister Princess Margaret; then a Prince and a Princess, elder children of the late Duke of Kent, and finally three more grandsons, all born during the last war—Princes William and Richard of Gloucester, born nearly three years apart, with Prince Michael of Kent coming in between. Then, only a few weeks after her youngest grandchild had celebrated his fourth birthday, Queen Mary became a great-grandmother with the birth of Prince Charles, the present Duke of Cornwall. Two years later came the birth of Princess Anne and, on her christening day, that of Viscount Lascelles, the first child of Queen Mary's eldest grandson.

Queen Mary has always been an immense success as a grandmother. Her grandchildren have shown the same veneration for her that an earlier generation felt for Queen Victoria, but their love has been unmarred by the barrier of awe, verging upon fear, which the old Queen always inspired in her descendants. Queen Mary has a peculiar understanding of young people, due perhaps to that remarkable memory of hers which thus bridges the gulf of three-quarters of a century and enables her to recall how she once felt in the days when she, too, was very young. To her friends it has sometimes seemed that, like many great Victorian women, she has shown herself more indulgent to her grandchildren than she was to her children in their young days, although this may be only another way of saying that she has moved with the times. Then, too, whereas Mamma was responsible for instilling all the early lessons in discipline, a visit from Grandmamma, or the privilege of calling upon her, is regarded as something of a special treat. One Royal Family custom, however, is observed as punctiliously as ever. Whenever they meet Queen Mary all her young relatives curtsey or bow before holding up their faces to be kissed.

Although in many families it is the girls rather than their brothers who are most attentive and responsive to grandmammas, Queen Mary has always been immensely popular with small boys. As the only sister of three brothers and the mother of five sons she has acquired and retained a deep insight into the juvenile male's outlook on life. Many of the toys which her young grandsons (and her great-grandson, Prince Charles) have displayed with most pride were presents from the royal grandmamma who has never, never, committed the unpardonable error of offering a young man who had reached the mature age of, say, three years something suitable only for girls or babies. She always chose instead a sturdy pedal toy, which not only developed good muscles but also gave its owner a gratifying sense of adult locomotion, or a push-cart on well-built wheels, which enabled a toddler to busy himself with a useful job of work, carrying this or that from here to there, while at the same time perfecting his mastery of the tricky technique of balance. When, on State occasions, the children were allowed to join the royal party to watch a great parade, the young princes rejoiced in a grandmother who

THE FAMILIAR BALCONY SCENE

Watching the Trooping of the Colour in 1951, Queen Mary draws the attention of little Prince Charles to the parade. Prince Richard of Gloucester watches enthralled.

not only shared a small boy's fascinated interest in "the soldiers," but also had much valuable information to impart about their history and their uniforms and all their other exciting paraphernalia, together with some handy tips as to how the various regiments could be identified.

There were other delights which particularly appealed to small girls, such as admiring Queen Mary's collection of dolls and miniature objects and the wonderful accumulation of silks, originally presented to her, from which, as they grew old enough to enjoy beautiful clothes, she sometimes gave them a dress length, doubly welcome in the days of coupons. There was her even more dazzling collection of jewellery, each piece telling a small chapter in royal history, and from this treasure, too, Queen Mary has made gifts to her granddaughters since they have been of an age to wear handsome jewels—the present Queen's favourite diamond tiara, for instance, was such a gift.

Queen Mary has always kept in the closest contact with all her grandchildren, right from the days when she first inspected them in their cradles, through the years when she received them escorted by their nannies and was consulted by their parents on each stage of their education, until the present time when the older members of the new generation turn to her for advice on the problems of adult life. She has always treated her young relatives as responsible little citizens. In the royal nurseries, where her influence was always so greatly to be seen, the baby talk for which she had scant use was rarely heard, while the smallest occupants have, with rare exceptions, always been addressed by their full and proper Christian names. Queen Mary, who has in many ways so much in common with Queen Victoria, never acquired her habit of burdening her descendants

PRINCESS ALEXANDRA DRIVES WITH QUEEN MARY

Princess Alexandra accompanies Queen Mary to the wedding reception of the Earl of Harewood.

QUEEN MARY AND HER GRANDSON
A charming and informal picture of Queen Mary with Prince Michael of Kent.

with absurd pet names which clung to them even when they were grown up.

Most of Queen Mary's activities as a grandmother have been conducted in the privacy of the family circle. The two daughters of the late King were, however, often seen in public with her from an early age, for she played an important part in the wider education and training for public life both of the present Queen and of the younger sister who was for so many years next to her in the line of succession to the Crown. She not only carefully scrutinized their schoolroom curriculum, but also drew up, to supplement their more formal instruction, a programme of afternoon outings to museums, galleries and other places of interest which were none the less entertaining by virtue of the fact that, with Queen Mary as guide, they were also highly educational.

This training of the little Princess who has now become our Queen, and the wise and kindly influence which is already watching over the early upbringing of the small Prince Charles who is now become heir-apparent, are not the least of Queen Mary's contributions to the future history of Britain and the world. It is but natural, therefore, that when the world hears mention of her grandchildren it thinks first of the present Queen and her sister, and when it hears of her great-grandson it thinks first of Prince Charles. But within the Royal Family circle there was never any such distinction, and Queen Mary remains the equally loving and equally beloved grandmother of all the royal cousins.

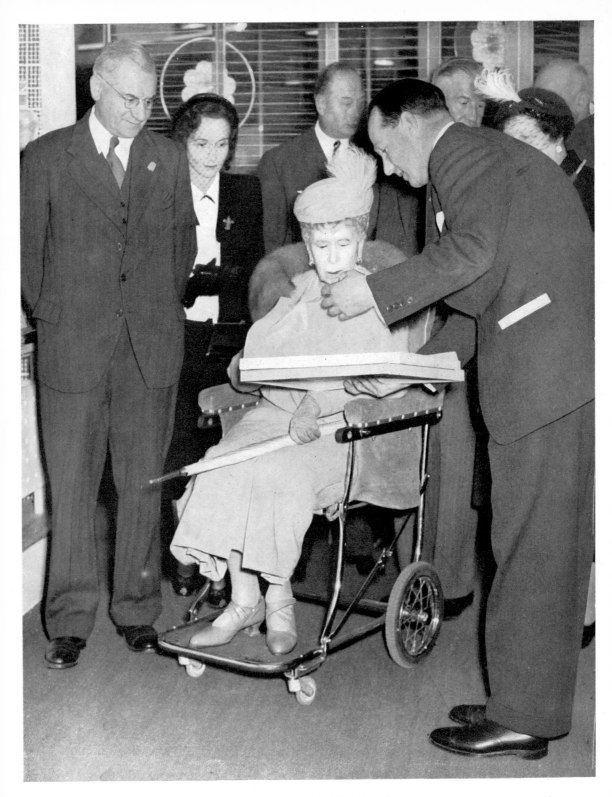

QUEEN MARY AT THE B.I.F.

British industry is one of Queen Mary's greatest interests, and she has rarely missed attending the British Industries Fair since its inauguration. She is seen here, at the age of eighty-four, inspecting an exhibit during a customarily thorough tour.

QUEEN MARY'S MANY INTERESTS

f royalty were called upon to enumerate their special interests, as are the distinguished persons who follow them in the pages of *Who's Who*, one wonders how Queen Mary's entry would read. Would it consist of a list of almost all the activities which occupy the leisure hours of her fellow men and women? Or would she, perhaps, with her gift for the terse, expressive phrase, extend her well-known love of economy to the saving of both words and paper and simply state "everything"?

When one comes to turn the pages of the great invisible scrapbook wherein our own memories and the reminiscences of our elders have written the history of the present times, it seems that there is almost nothing in which Queen Mary has not taken an interest. Certainly all the items in that proverbially comprehensive catalogue— "shoes and ships and sealing-wax, cabbages and kings"—have all at one time or another claimed her attention. It would be much simpler, one feels, to compile a short list of the few matters in which she has never been greatly interested. This would include most forms of sport (with an exception in favour of lawn tennis). Racing appeals to her only to the extent that she has enjoyed attending such major events of the course as Royal Ascot and the Derby, regarding these rather as great national and social occasions than as purely sporting functions. In shooting, that other favourite sport of British kings, she has no personal interest beyond the fact that walking with the guns provided her with a pleasant opportunity of enjoying the countryside, while the contents of the bags made an acceptable addition to the table. It would be a gross libel to say that Queen Mary was not fond of animals, since she is far too British to be anything but kind to all living things and far too sensitive to tolerate any form of cruelty. Yet pets have never played the prominent part in her life which they do in the lives of most of her fellow-countrymen and women. But with these few exceptions it is difficult to find any subject on which Queen Mary cannot talk with the authority and enthusiasm of one who has made it a special study.

Queen Mary is a collector, and not merely in the connoisseur's sense of the word, for her "collections" are not limited to the fine furniture, china, pictures and other works of art which fill her home. She has always collected all manner of other things in the same way as a schoolboy might collect matchbox lids or—in less austere days— cigarette cards. She has, for instance, a vast and ever-growing collection of fascinating miniature objects, the work of nineteenth-century craftsmen. Most of these are

Victorian, although some were skilfully fashioned out of odds and ends by the prisoners brought here during the Napoleonic wars. She has added to her collection by purchases made at curio shops all over the country or at charity bazaars, and also by gifts from those who have heard of her interest. Sometimes she meets a fellow enthusiast unexpectedly, for this is a hobby open to those of modest means and limited housing space. A year or two ago, for example, she visited the New Lindsey Theatre, where the veteran actress, Miss Nancy Price, presented her schoolgirl granddaughter to Queen Mary, who, with her quick insight into the minds of others and especially young people, soon discovered that she was addressing a fellow collector. A day or two later she went through her own accumulation at Marlborough House and chose a tiny model violin, a selection of wee china and glass ornaments and one or two other pieces, packed these carefully in a box with cotton-wool, added a note in her own handwriting setting forth the details of the contents and had the parcel sent to the theatre as a present from an octogenarian Queen to a young schoolgirl who shared her own delightful hobby.

Most women of her generation accumulated family photographs, but few people have ever "collected" these in the same systematic way as Queen Mary. Her impressive series of albums contains a pictorial record of every member of the family for several generations—studio portraits, snapshots taken by relatives and friends, and press photographs recording almost every public appearance which she and her husband ever made. Many of these are captioned, sometimes amusingly, in her own handwriting.

One odd item which Queen Mary collected in her young days was cast horseshoes found by herself. In the years when these were a commoner sight on country roads than they are today she would often stop her carriage or car to retrieve a specimen which her sharp eyes had noticed by the wayside. This was one of the few superstitious customs which Queen Mary ever observed. In the small family museum at Sandringham there are a number of these pieces of old iron whose labels record that they were found by her at places as far apart as Salisbury Plain and Canada.

For most of the world the day of small homes and labour-saving policy has meant an end to that most fascinating of all collections, the souvenirs of red-letter days and other special events. Queen Mary has always treasured these reminders of bygone days: the dance and concert programmes, the order of ceremony, the menus of banquets, as well as the small trifles which she has picked up on her travels. Although all her collections are valuable—if only by virtue of the fact that they belong to her—some have also a considerable intrinsic worth. She has, for instance, one of the most comprehensive collections of fans in existence, some specimens having been painted by royal artists. Unlike many collectors, Queen Mary is generous in parting with even a highly-prized acquisition, particularly when she feels that she is thus restoring it to its rightful historical background. When visiting Blenheim Palace during the war, for instance, she presented the Duchess of Marlborough with a fan illustrating the old French song, "*Marlbrouk s'en va-t-en guerre.*"

QUEEN MARY PLANTS A TREE

By royal custom Queen Mary planted a tree to commemorate her visit, with King George V, to Yorkshire in 1923, for the christening at Goldsborough Church of their eldest grandson.

While most of Queen Mary's treasures reflect her appreciation of the art and craftsmanship of an earlier age, her flower pictures include those of contemporary artists. She has a great liking for this type of painting, and for many years has made it her custom to have a favourite flower or garden picture reproduced on her personal Christmas card.

Throughout her long life she has always found great happiness and solace in times of sorrow and anxiety in lovely gardens, and in days of crisis she and her husband would often stroll for an hour or more in the grounds of Buckingham Palace. She has often observed (as do her descendants) the charming royal custom, which was already well established in her youth, of planting a tree to mark her visits. When she stayed at Sandringham for the first time after her eightieth birthday she planted, to commemorate this landmark in her life, a small oak tree on the lawn in front of the house where almost every tree bears its label recording that it was planted by some royal guest.

The royal gardens, like the residences they surround, owe much to Queen Mary, who planned them as the background of her homes, occasionally having a tree or two felled to open a vista, but more often clearing away the dreary undergrowth of

A QUEEN'S HOBBIES

Her flowers and her needlework are two quiet pleasures which have remained with Queen Mary through many years. She combines the two as she works at her gros point *out-of-doors in the garden.*

"evergreens" to make a colourful shrubbery or a little shel-
tered corner. When she lived at
Buckingham Palace the early
weeks of the year always found
her hunting the first snowdrop
in the "wilderness" which she
had made there, for she has
always loved shy little flowers
as much as any handsome
product of the nurseryman's
art. She has, however, admired
many of the achievements and
improvements of present-day
horticulture, and the Chelsea
Flower Show has been one of
the annual engagements which
she has rarely missed. She is the
gardener's delight, for when
discussing any plant she is
always able to give it its correct
name, mentioning the variety
which she has in mind and not
merely referring to a rose or a
delphinium. She likes to decide
the planting schemes for her
own delightful walled garden
at Marlborough House, and
when, shortly after the last war,

THE QUEEN AND THE GARDENER

*Queen Mary talks of gardening with an allotment holder
during a visit to Datchet in 1919.*

she received a present of tulip bulbs from the people of Holland, she helped to plant
these out herself.

In the smaller matters of life, as well as in its larger issues, Queen Mary has always
contrived to reconcile the love of tradition with a progressive outlook. Although she
has never accepted novelty as a commendation in itself, she has always been willing to
investigate, and often to experiment with, the latest improvements in any sphere.
When she and King George V heard of the wonderful advances in size and colour
range which had been achieved in the development of that favourite dweller in the old-
fashioned herbaceous border, the common lupin, by a horticulturist named George
Russell, the royal gardener was sent to offer him any sum within reason for some seed.
But Mr. Russell, who before he died in 1951 at the age of ninety-four had achieved

AT THE CHELSEA FLOWER SHOW

Queen Mary shares her knowledge of flowers with W.V.S. members who exhibited this model garden.

world-wide fame with his lupins, had so far refused to part with his precious seed and the messenger returned empty-handed. The royal gardens would have had long to wait for their magnificent display of multi-coloured lupins had not Queen Mary taken the matter into her own hands. She sent a personal message to Mr. Russell, telling him how much she and the King had admired some specimens which they had seen and how anxious they were to establish some of the plants in their garden. That autumn both seeds and plants arrived at Buckingham Palace; they were the first specimens with which their "creator" had ever parted.

Flowers have always meant more to Queen Mary than a merely conventional form of indoor decoration or a convenient offering to accompany a message of goodwill or sympathy. Flowers are as much a part of her home as any of her treasures, and she likes to sit and work surrounded by well-filled vases whose contents she selects as carefully as any of her more permanent possessions, choosing them for their fragrance and their beauty of colour. She has never restricted herself to the formal white floral decorations which were favoured in the days of her Victorian youth.

Like all people for whom flowers fill such a genuine need that they rank almost as one of the essentials of life, she often sends a bouquet or a growing plant to her friends, believing that they will bring the same happiness to others as they do to her. To the sick or elderly whose days are bounded by the four walls of a room, or to those whose work rarely allows them to escape beyond the London pavements and chimney-pots, her gifts of flowers bring lasting joy, for even if the blossoms are short-lived their memory never fades. Friends of one of the early women trade-union leaders still recall how they always knew when Queen Mary had visited her at her little house in Bloomsbury. The royal visitor would always bring at least one and often a whole row of flowering plants. When Queen Mary is sending cut flowers to the sick or aged, who may have no one available to arrange them, she sometimes sends them in a vase (when the destination is sufficiently near for the gift to be delivered by her chauffeur) with a note asking for this to be filled up immediately with water. It was Queen Mary, too, who established the custom of sending to hospitals the daffodils grown on the slopes at Windsor, and when in residence at the Castle in the spring she would gather them herself with the help of her ladies-in-waiting. In recent years, when she has had more leisure than she once possessed, Queen Mary has often made the enjoyment of some particularly lovely floral display the incentive for her afternoon drive. Some seasons, when she would not otherwise have been at Windsor in time to see the daffodils at their

THE QUEEN'S WORK ON SHOW

At the first post-war exhibition of the Royal School of Needlework, Queen Mary saw some of her own work displayed. It included an exquisitely-worked panelled screen in gros point.

best, she has driven there expressly to enjoy them. She often goes to Kew Gardens in time for the bluebells and the cherry blossom, while one of her favourite London outings is to Regent's Park, where, unrecognized, she will descend from her car to stand quietly among the roses, admiring their beauty and enjoying their fragrance, in the garden which is named after her.

Another of Queen Mary's great interests, which, like her love of flowers and gardens, dates from her girlhood years, is the theatre. Her parents never carried into their private life that official condemnation of the stage which banned actors and actresses from appearing at Court. Henry Irving and Ellen Terry were frequent visitors at their home and were thus two of the great theatrical personalities whom Queen Mary met long before her marriage. Sometimes, when she was old enough, her mother would take her to the famous supper parties which Sir Henry Irving gave on the stage of the Lyceum after the show was over. Visits to the theatre were not confined, in her family, to attendance at gala performances, to be regarded as brilliant social functions rather than opportunities to enjoy a play. Queen Mary's mother had never, unless owing to prolonged absence abroad, missed any new play of importance in the London theatre since the 1850s, and her daughter carried on the tradition, in later years extending her patronage to the smaller and less-well-known theatres outside the fashionable West End.

It was not until King George V and Queen Mary had been on the throne for several years that any actress was permitted to appear at Court, other than in a professional capacity at a Command Performance. This banishment led to a difficult situation when, at the beginning of the reign, the King's Librarian, the great military historian, Sir John Fortescue, married an actress. During the periods of the Sovereign's residence at Windsor Castle (then more frequent than they have become in recent years) Sir John was necessarily a member of the Household-in-Waiting, and in the normal way his wife would have accompanied him to all the social functions to which he was invited by the King and Queen. Realizing that this would involve an infringement of the long-standing rule, and not wishing to cause embarrassment, his wife had arranged that at such times she would remain at their London home.

On the Court's first visit to Windsor after their marriage, Queen Mary called at the Librarian's residence at the Castle. Sir John received her alone, explaining that his wife was in London. The Queen left almost immediately, and he had the impression, so he told his wife later, that she was somewhat "put out" at not finding the lady of the house at home. It was therefore decided that Lady Fortescue had better join her husband at Windsor, in case the Queen called again. Queen Mary did make a second visit, and almost the first question which she asked her hostess was: "Were you really away from home last time I called?" "But of course, Ma'am, I was in London as my husband explained to you," she was assured. Queen Mary replied in her forthright way that when she had been shown into the room on the previous occasion she had noticed a piece of half-worked embroidery, with the needle dangling from its thread, showing that it had obviously been hurriedly cast aside when she had been announced. It was only then that the Queen discovered, to her intense amusement and delight, that her husband's learned Librarian had long found relaxation from his scholarly researches in the gentle art of needlework.

Before she left, Queen Mary assured her host that she and her husband would always receive his wife in private. Not long afterwards Lady Fortescue and Ellen Terry became the first two actresses to be officially presented at Buckingham Palace.

West End theatres are, of course, accustomed to honouring royal visitors in the approved style, but Queen Mary's excursions into the less fashionable realms of drama have occasionally brought her an amusing insight into the more homely aspects of theatrical life. When she visited the "Old Vic" in the great days when Lilian Baylis reigned over this pioneer theatre of the people with her loving, turbulent and highly individual despotism, even the bouquet was "different." This little formality had been overlooked until the very last moment, when a messenger, hurriedly sent out to the adjacent street market in the "Cut" to drive the best bargain he could on behalf of an establishment which had always had to count its ha'pence, had returned with a generous

THE QUEEN MEETS BALLET STARS
The theatre in all its aspects has been of lifelong interest to Queen Mary, who enjoys meeting and talking to the artistes. She is here with Alicia Markova and Anton Dolin at the 1951 Festival Ballet.

but somewhat windblown bunch of chrysanthemums. Towards the end of the performance Miss Baylis, who was always happier when free to wander from pit to gallery than when confined to the stage box, remarked with a sigh of relief: "Well, Ma'am, they'll soon be playing your husband's tune"—an apposite if novel description of the National Anthem.

During the reign of King George V and Queen Mary the phrase "Command Performance" took on a new significance. The old custom of summoning a complete West End company to perform, before a private audience at one of the royal residences, the production which it normally gave in public was abandoned, largely owing to the heavy expense involved. The new conception of a Command Performance as a specially devised programme, in which artistes of outstanding merit were honoured by the presence of the King and his family at a London theatre, marked a further stage in the happy relationship between the Crown and what was at last recognized as a fine and honourable profession.

Another step forward came with the discovery that royal audiences did not necessarily require an act to be censored for their benefit. When King George and his Consort, as Prince and Princess of Wales, attended a variety show at Hoxton, one of the greatest comedians of the day was instructed to rehearse a slightly abridged version of his turn and promise faithfully not to depart from this lest he give offence to the royal guests and particularly to Queen Mary, who was suspected of being rather less broad-minded than the majority of her husband's subjects. But, in the tremendous enthusiasm which swept the house on the night, the comedian forgot all about the special version and threw himself heart and soul into delivering his normal robust and slightly vulgar turn. The stage manager, watching from the wings, shuddered at the prospect of royal disapproval, but those who glanced across at the guests of honour observed King George rocking with laughter, while his wife was apparently equally amused.

Queen Mary always appreciated the homely humour of the old-style comedians and held many of the stars of music-hall heyday in as high an esteem as she did the leading actors and actresses of the legitimate stage. When she learnt that the veteran comedienne, Kate Carney, was celebrating her eightieth birthday a few years ago, she sent her a message of congratulation from Sandringham, where she was spending her holiday at the time, drawing attention in her letter to the fact that their two ages were almost the same. More recently, on learning that her own doctors were attending George Formby during his serious illness, she entrusted them with an encouraging message telling him "not to work so hard."

During her married life Queen Mary, like other members of the Royal Family, almost always occupied a box when she visited the theatre, but in later years she has often preferred to sit in the stalls with the general public, the tickets for her small party being booked by telephone at short notice. Her recommendation has frequently led her

QUEEN MARY AT FILM PREMIÈRE

Queen Mary meets the director—Mr. Charles Crichton—at a charity première of The Lavender Hill Mob. *With her is Mr. J. Arthur Rank.*

younger relatives, including the present Queen, to see a play which they might otherwise have missed. As always, Queen Mary is interested in the people as well as their work, and she usually sends for two or three members of the cast to come and chat to her in the intervals.

Although Queen Mary has never shown the same liking for the cinema that she has for the stage, it was during the reign of King George V that private film showings, now a regular feature of royal life, were first introduced in the royal homes as a form of entertainment. The staff were, as now, allowed to attend and, at Sandringham and Balmoral particularly, both of which are, from a Londoner's point of view, very benighted areas and far from cinemas, this has proved a most welcome amenity. When Queen Mary selected the first series of films for the inauguration of these private showings she asked for a Mickey Mouse to be included, and this item amused her so much that in subsequent programmes at least one cartoon was always shown as well as newsreels and the main feature.

Queen Mary's visits to public cinemas have not been entirely confined to charity

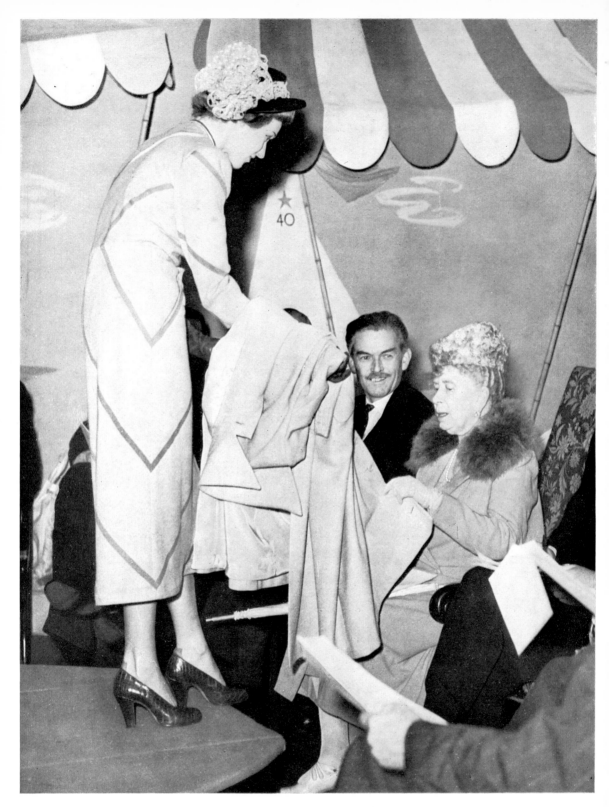

THE QUEEN AT A FASHION SHOW

Queen Mary, who throughout her long public life has supported faithfully the British clothing industry,
inspects with interest a coat displayed at a 1949 show organized by the International Wool Secretariat.

premières. From time to time she has made a private visit to see a more serious type of film and then she has simply occupied a seat at the back of the stalls. Occasionally, when she has missed the West End showing of some film which she particularly wanted to see, she has viewed it after its release at a suburban cinema.

Not all Queen Mary's interests are highly intellectual; one which she shares with most women is that fascinating pastime of "going round the shops," and not merely setting forth expressly to purchase something. Queen Mary was a pioneer among royal shoppers, for until her reign it was considered that etiquette required a Queen to summon all her tradesmen to wait upon her. For all articles of personal apparel which demand fittings Queen Mary has always made her selection and given her orders within the privacy of her own home. But for presents or household purchases she has always liked to shop herself. She also encouraged her children—and later generations of royal youngsters—to visit the shops so that they might see how much things cost and learn to understand the value of money. Although Queen Mary's visits to large stores were, for the general convenience, always notified to the management in advance, she insisted that other customers must not be excluded on her account. On more than one occasion when she was being taken up in a lift and the operator was about to shut the gate on other shoppers, Queen Mary quietly remarked: "There is plenty of room," and gestured for those who were waiting to share her ride. Shoppers saw her as the modest and human woman she always has been in private life. Once, on emerging from a store, she noticed a small child who had become separated from its mother, and she gently took it by the hand and restored it to parental control.

Queen Mary has more than an interest in history; she possesses the rare gift of a true historical instinct, which is responsible not for one but for many of her interests. She has always liked visiting museums, not merely to inspect their contents but to observe how these were displayed and how much enthusiasm they aroused in others. She has always been particularly fascinated by the things which were associated with individual people; she "knew" the dead-and-gone members of the Royal Family, whom she had never even seen, so well that more than once she was able to point out that a bust or portrait was wrongly labelled; she several times discovered that curators had confused the various sons of her great-grandfather, George III. She has visited not only the well-known places of interest, like Westminster Abbey and the Tower of London, but also those where many people would have said "there was not much to see," such as the foundations of the old Whitehall Palace which came to light during a demolition scheme. If she has read in her morning newspaper about any such discovery within a reasonable distance she has often determined to go along and inspect it, and only once, so far, has she been thwarted. She had learnt that some interesting old houses had been uncovered in the course of a clearance near one of the Thames wharves, and she decided to inspect these for herself without delay. When, however, her lady-in-waiting made the necessary telephone inquiries, it was found that the buildings were in such a highly dangerous condition and so difficult of access that no one, not even Queen Mary herself, could be admitted.

Usually Queen Mary's visits, unless she has chosen to arrive entirely unannounced, have been heralded by a telephone call. Occasionally, however, she has resorted to other means. One day, finding herself within easy reach of Stanway, she decided that she would like to see over this historic Cotswold home of the Wemyss family, which was at one time the summer retreat of the old Abbots of Tewkesbury. She found that the house was let to the late Sir James Barrie, that shyest and most elusive of celebrities. Sir James was given no opportunity to flee from the honour of a royal visit, for the local police sergeant, advised by telephone, arrived on the doorstep to announce that Queen Mary wished to call. Although the royal visitor came to see the house rather than its illustrious tenant, she remembered, with exquisite tact, to ask Barrie for the real solution of "Shall We Join the Ladies?", that famous one-act mystery play for which the author never found the answer.

Authors have found a special delight in meeting Queen Mary, for she does not merely assure them that she has read their books; she proceeds to give conclusive evidence that she has remembered them. Although she has always shown a great interest in history, biography, diaries and letters—books about people, in fact—her choice of literature is very wide. Sometimes she has visited her favourite London bookshop to spend an hour or so examining the latest books, arriving so unobtrusively and browsing among the shelves so quietly that other customers have either left without noticing her or have looked up suddenly and been astonished to find that they had been almost rubbing shoulders with a Queen.

Queen Mary studies the advance notices of forthcoming books, and occasionally when, in these post-war years, publication has been delayed for several months, her bookseller will receive an inquiry from Marlborough House asking whether a particular book has appeared yet.

Like many of the outstanding personalities of our day, Queen Mary enjoys detective stories, and although she is not a great radio fan, she also sometimes listens to a broadcast mystery play. Just as everyone else does, she likes to try to guess the solution, and when a year or two ago she went to the theatre to see one of Agatha Christie's plays she begged the author, who was presented to her during the interval, not to tell her "who had done it," as the book from which it was taken happened to be one of the few which she had not read.

The old-fashioned custom of reading aloud, once such a delightful feature of English home life, and now almost unknown, is still observed at Marlborough House. By getting her ladies-in-waiting to read either a book or a newspaper to her for several hours a day, Queen Mary is able to devote much time to her other favourite hobby, needlework, not strictly an indoor occupation with her, for in warm weather she likes to sit and do her embroidery in the garden. Her speciality in the last fifteen years or so

QUEEN MARY VISITS ROYAL SCHOOL OF NEEDLEWORK
The royal visitor examines with her usual interest the work of girls at the school.

has been *gros point* embroidery, which she finds less trying to her eyes than finer work, although she still sews and threads her own needles without glasses, merely using her lorgnette to inspect any intricate detail. Her work is prepared for her by the Royal School of Needlework, in which she has always taken a strong interest. Queen Mary chooses her patterns, usually a flower motif or period design, according to the purpose which the tapestry is destined to fulfil; a chair seat, for instance, or a panel for a screen. The canvas then comes to her ready-stamped, with the wools tidily slotted along the edges. She is an exquisitely neat worker, prides herself on always doing her own "tidying up" when she has finished, and keeps her current work in one of her several sewing bags from which she can always choose one to harmonize with her gown.

Other people's needlework interests her as well as her own, and when staying at

Sandringham she several times visited a famous collection of nineteenth-century embroidery which was housed in a local rectory. Queen Mary's Needlework Guild, now her "own" society but once her mother's favourite project, has already been mentioned in connexion with its astounding achievements during the First World War. Even when another war had come and gone, almost every autumn still found Queen Mary visiting its packing headquarters in Kensington to inspect the work and help pack the garments. This was no perfunctory visit of goodwill; in order to devote several consecutive hours to the task, the royal patron, often accompanied by her daughter, the Princess Royal, and one or two friends, would arrive complete with packed lunch so that she might be able to see the job well and truly completed before she had to hurry away to some other engagement.

The very active and conscientious patronage of many charities forms part of Queen Mary's public work, but it also infiltrates into her private life. She has always had a personal interest in the small individual enterprise—charity is too limited a word—which has resulted from a number of people of goodwill and energy getting together to meet some current need in their own way. The new approach to the age-old problem

FESTIVAL EXHIBITION OF GOLD AND SILVER

Queen Mary has an extensive knowledge and appreciation of beautiful things, and was an especially interested visitor to the Festival Exhibition of gold and silver at the Goldsmiths' Hall.

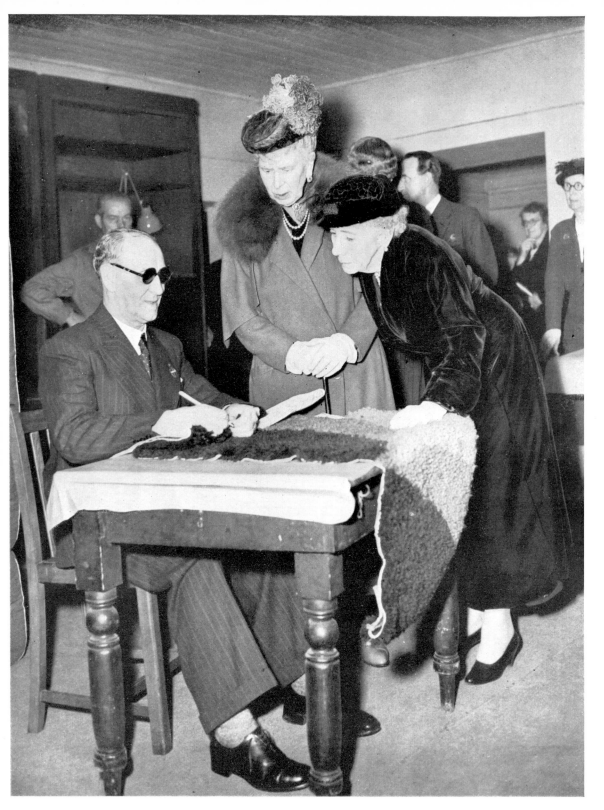

QUEEN MARY SEES DISABLED EX-SERVICEMEN AT WORK

*During a visit to the Lord Roberts Workshops at Kensington, Queen Mary stopped to watch a blind
rug-maker. Her interest in disabled workers is well known and she gives them much practical support.*

has always attracted her. The first baby crèche at Deptford and the pre-war Clubland Church of Walworth, which suffered so sadly in the blitz, were undertakings to which she gave more than is commonly expected of a royal patron. Indeed, to all "her" organizations she gives that little extra personal thought—the used Christmas cards which she collects from her family and friends and passes on to those who can make use of them; the fragrant lavender from Sandringham, where she spends her summer holiday, which goes, with her good wishes, to Queen Mary's Hospital for the East End at Stratford, as a reminder for the patients there of a lovely English garden; the copies of *Punch* which are regularly dispatched from Marlborough House to the same destination; all are proof of the fact that once Queen Mary has bestowed her patronage its recipients are never far from her mind. Each year she sends a special little Christmas donation of five or ten pounds to a score or so of charities, and this is but a fraction of her total of regular charitable donations. For years she has kept the Queen Mary's Maternity Home at Hampstead supplied with cot covers (pink for girls and blue for boys) crocheted by herself, and when, a year or so ago, she called in at the Home unexpectedly she noticed that these were well-worn and faded with constant laundering

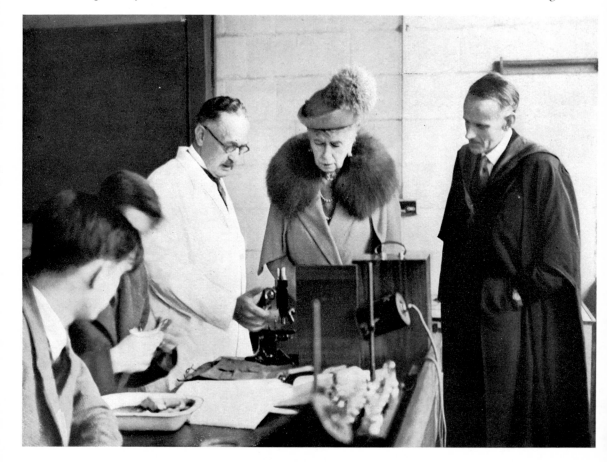

VISITING THE QUEEN MARY COLLEGE

At the college which bears her name Queen Mary saw students at work and inspected with interest a microscope in the Zoology Department.

QUEEN MARY SEES HOW A WATCH WORKS

As one who always likes to "see for herself," Queen Mary took great interest in the enlarged mechanism of a watch displayed at the B.I.F.

and immediately remarked in her practical way: "I must make some more for you."

The rest of the world, the great majority of us who can never find time for this or are always putting off that to some less busy day which never seems to arrive, can only marvel how Queen Mary, still active in public and family life at the age of eighty-five, could and still can accomplish so much in one lifetime. The answer from those who watch her daily routine with love and admiration is that she abhors the wasted moment just as much as she abhors a waste of food or money. Her day is organized from her early rising until her eleven-o'clock bedtime, which, for a great-grandmother, is not so early; she decides at exactly what hour each event shall take place, and she is never a minute late, even for a solitary meal in her own home.

As a young married woman she made this orderly punctuality her plan for living and it has remained ever since; for her a lifelong habit, for the Royal Family and households a legacy from one who by sheer force of will has always imparted to others the discipline which she has imposed upon herself.

105

THE CORONATION OF GEORGE VI

Queen Mary set a royal precedent when, as Queen Mother, she attended her son's Coronation in 1937.

QUEEN MARY—QUEEN MOTHER

The last entry in King George V's diary records, in Queen Mary's elegant handwriting, that at his request she had entered up the journal of her beloved husband when he was no longer able to hold the pen himself. On a January day in 1936 a great King breathed his last in the quiet land of Norfolk that he loved, and Queen Mary, after more than a quarter of a century, was Queen Consort no longer. She was not, at first, to be known as Queen Mother, for there was no other Queen. The new King, whose hand she kissed as she knelt to pay him a first private homage beside his father's deathbed, had no wife. But before the year was out she was to kiss the hand of another son, so suddenly become King George VI, whose accession, with his wife Elizabeth as Queen, was to bestow upon Queen Mary the title of Queen Mother. Less than sixteen years later she was to drive to Clarence House to pay the same tribute to her granddaughter, newly returned from Africa, to whom she had already written, signing herself "Your loving Grandmother and subject." So many centuries have passed since a Consort lived to see her grandchild on the throne that there was no traditional title for a Queen who was also a grandmother. The former Queen Elizabeth has become Queen Mother and the Consort of King George V is once again simply Queen Mary, the proudest and most beautiful of the many names by which she has been known.

As King Edward VIII continued, until the last few weeks of his reign, to reside at York House, which had been his home as Prince of Wales, it was not until the autumn of 1936 that Queen Mary left Buckingham Palace. She then moved to Marlborough House, taking with her her private possessions, her own Household, most of whose members had already served her for many years past, and King George V's little dog. Since that day, whenever Queen Mary has been in London her personal standard has flown from the great red-brick mansion overlooking the Mall where she lived as Princess of Wales, and where in her childhood days of three-quarters of a century ago she had often visited the little "Waleses" of the day, one of whom was to become her husband.

Owing to Court mourning observed for King George V, 1936 was for Queen Mary a comparatively uneventful year—at least to outward appearance—as far as her public activities were concerned. But within the royal homes these were momentous months, fraught with an anxiety which the nation was soon to share. Throughout this time Queen Mary was, in the words of one of her Household, a "tower of strength" to her family. As the Abdication crisis broke upon the world her children turned to her, visiting her constantly, seeking not only her advice but the spiritual support of her

QUEEN MARY AND HER ELDEST SON

The Duke of Windsor with Queen Mary during one of his occasional visits to this country.

wisdom, serenity and love. She lived very quietly during those last troubled days of the brief reign of her eldest son, holding herself always ready to receive her children at whatever hour they might need to call upon her. To others she spoke little of all that was uppermost in her own mind and the minds of those around her, and she was never heard to say anything which could betoken criticism or impatience or any thought of self. She hoped and prayed only for what was best for her country and its sovereignty and for the son who was still also her King. When all was settled she drove across to see her daughter-in-law who was soon to become Queen and who was, at the time, ill in bed at her home in Piccadilly. On 12 December King George VI was proclaimed, and shortly afterwards Queen Mary joined the new Sovereign and his family at Sandringham for the traditional royal Christmas.

Although the former King, under his new title of Duke of Windsor, went into voluntary exile within a few hours of his abdication, he remained in the closest possible touch with his family and especially with his mother. Whenever he returned to his own country his first act was always to visit her at Marlborough House. At first there were those who, with mistaken tact, sought to spare Queen Mary by suppressing any reminder of the short reign which had come to so untimely an end. Gently, yet so firmly, she let it be understood that history could not thus be re-written by attempting to expunge from the memory of the nation he no longer ruled as King the records of one who had served so faithfully as Prince of Wales. By so doing she helped to restore a proper sense of proportion to confused public opinion, setting before others the wise example of her own well-balanced mind.

Queen Mary will always be remembered as a great upholder of tradition, and yet she has also set many precedents. Until 1937 it was not considered correct for a Queen Dowager to see her successor crowned. Queen Adelaide, hearing at Marlborough House the gunfire which heralded Queen Victoria's arrival at Westminster Abbey, had written to her young niece regretting that "I must address you in writing" and "cannot take part in the sacred ceremony of your Coronation." Queen Alexandra had stayed at Sandringham while her son was crowned King George V in London. There was, however, no logical reason why a Queen Dowager should not attend the Coronation of a new Sovereign, while there was every reason for a mother wishing to share with her child and other members of her family in this the greatest of all State occasions. Queen Mary's stately figure, clad in her purple velvet robes, was there to add grace to her son's Coronation procession, and later to appear upon the Palace

CORONATION BALCONY SCENE, 1937

Queen Mary waves to the crowds during a family balcony appearance after the Coronation.

START OF THE ROYAL TOUR, 1939

*When King George VI and Queen Elizabeth left for their Canadian tour in May, 1939, they were
seen off at Waterloo by their little daughters and by Queen Mary, in whose care the Princesses were left.*

balcony before those vast crowds in whose eyes no royal occasion could be complete without her presence.

In the two remaining years of peace Queen Mary created a new place for a Queen Mother in the life of the nation, just as she had in former years given a new meaning to the title of Queen Consort. Her public appearances were not regarded as some sweet, nostalgic reminder of the past; she belonged, as she still does, to the present. When, in 1939, the King and Queen paid their State visit to Canada and the U.S.A., Queen Mary took over a special responsibility for the care of the young Princesses who, while they remained at Buckingham Palace, frequently visited their grandmother and accompanied her on a number of informal visits to places of interest. Queen Mary, more than any other member of the Royal Family, is a true Londoner, not merely in the sense that she was born in London, but because she knows and loves her capital city in a way which few of its citizens can rival. It was, therefore, with much reluctance that she agreed, in the event of war, to become an "evacuee." It was only her desire to

QUEEN MARY AND PRINCESSES TOUR LONDON DOCKS
Queen Mary took her granddaughters to many places of interest, including London Docks.

spare the King, her son, all unnecessary anxiety, and also her commonsense appreciation of the burden which her presence in London would impose upon police and others responsible for her safety, which reconciled her to leaving her home.

For more than five years, until the end of the war in Europe, Queen Mary made her home at Badminton, one of the great English country houses which she had always loved so well and whose owner, the Duke of Beaufort, had married her niece, the former Lady Mary Cambridge. In the historic West Country mansion Queen Mary had her own separate quarters where she installed her Household and staff, both greatly reduced in size with so many of the members serving in the Forces. Much of her normal public work was necessarily curtailed. Annual events which she had attended for years past were suspended "for the duration," while the places which she had visited so regularly in the past were now beyond her reach. But Queen Mary never entertained the idea of enforced retirement. At the age of seventy-two she methodically set about creating a new life for herself in the West of England.

Queen Mary, who, with her life-long habit of "getting things done," would have found a thousand useful jobs to do had she been marooned at the North Pole or in the midst of the Sahara, found no lack of scope in the immediate vicinity of Badminton. She soon made friends with the little evacuee London children and organized them into "weeding parties." She found occupations for the small contingent of military dispatch riders who were stationed there in order to conduct her, should need arise, to a yet safer retreat. Anyone who had, for the moment, nothing to do was recruited into one of her "wooding parties" to collect fuel to help out the coal ration. Queen Mary herself, saw in hand, clad in sensible shoes and well-worn tweeds, would tackle the smaller, lower boughs, while the men carted the heavier logs to the waiting lorry. She also showed the youngsters how to gather kindling in neat bundles.

She regarded idleness as almost a criminal offence. In the evening she would sit with her sewing or knitting, and even the male members of the Household were expected to provide themselves with "work." One distinguished courtier, rebelling against the prospect of yet another evening's knitting, occasionally contrived to "forget" his needles and wool, but the Queen always noticed his idle fingers and inquired, with a twinkle in her eye, what had become of his "work."

Queen Mary herself spent a busy life attending troops' concerts (where she often joined in the singing), visiting canteens (and sometimes fulfilling a soldier's order for "a nice cup of char, please Ma") and inspecting all kinds of war work. When she learnt that workers at some of the smaller factories felt overlooked, because the King and Queen and other members of the Royal Family touring the country naturally tended to concentrate on the more important industrial centres, she planned out programmes which would enable her to visit many of the small workshops within reach. She was also a constant visitor to local hospitals. War gave a new impetus to her lifelong campaign against waste. A leading industrialist once spoke of her "by-product mind," and wherever she went Queen Mary was always inquiring whether everything was being used to the best advantage, from domestic salvage to the leisure hours of women tied to their homes by family duties. Characteristically, for she has always endeavoured to practise what she preached, she was one of the first car owners to instruct her chauffeur that no serviceman or woman thumbing a lift should ever be ignored if there was a spare seat in her car, regardless of whether or not she herself were travelling in it at the time. In the early days of the war soldiers and airmen who returned to their units and assured their colleagues that they had driven with the King's mother in her car were often accused of "shooting a line." So Queen Mary, who always understood how much pride and pleasure ordinary people derived from a chance meeting with one of the Royal Family, had small medals struck with her initial on them and gave one as a souvenir to each of her casual passengers.

These years, when Queen Mary's official address, as passed by the censor, was

QUEEN MARY AND HER "WOODING PARTY"
No one was idle on the Badminton estate—soldiers recruited to collect fuel had the Queen as a leader.

MRS. ROOSEVELT VISITS QUEEN MARY

One of Queen Mary's guests at Badminton was Mrs. Eleanor Roosevelt, wife of the then President of the U.S.A. They posed for this picture with the Princess Royal and the Duke and Duchess of Beaufort.

"somewhere in the country," were by no means uneventful. Her family, including her grandchildren, visited her whenever they could, while she joined them occasionally when, for instance, they spent Christmas at Windsor Castle. At Badminton she received many distinguished visitors, including the exiled heads of allied countries, who found that Queen Mary, despite her country retreat, was always one of the best-informed people in the land. One of her guests, Mrs. Eleanor Roosevelt, wife of the then President of the U.S.A., remarked to her that she had discovered in Britain no women who still led an entirely social life. "Of course not," replied Queen Mary firmly. "There would be no one for them to lead it with here."

It was at Badminton that Queen Mary received the sad tidings of the death of her youngest surviving son, the late Duke of Kent, who was killed on active service in 1942, when the aeroplane in which he was travelling on duty crashed in Scotland.

Queen Mary was sitting one night after dinner, busy as usual with her "work," when the telephone call came from Balmoral, where the late King had just been informed of his brother's death. Queen Mary at once retired to her room, for it was too late to do anything that night, but she ordered her car to be ready early next

WARTIME VISIT TO WOOLLEN MILLS

Even her wartime "exile" from London did nothing to lessen Queen Mary's active interest in the industrial life of the country. She is seen here during a visit to the Witney Mills in 1941.

THE FAMOUS "DOLLAR CARPET"
This picture of one of the twelve panels of the carpet shows the exquisitely-worked eighteenth-century flower design executed in gros point. Queen Mary's signature is in the lower right-hand corner.

morning so that she could make the long journey right across the south of England to comfort her bereaved goddaughter and daughter-in-law, the Duchess of Kent.

In the previous year, 1941, Queen Mary began the famous "Dollar Carpet" which, although it is only one of many which she has worked, is now celebrated all over the world. It took her more than eight years to embroider the twelve panels, each adorned with a different eighteenth-century flower design, and the decorative floral border, and as each section was finished she embroidered her signature and the date in one corner. When she first began making the carpet, which measures 10 feet 2 inches by 6 feet $9\frac{1}{2}$ inches, she had intended it for Windsor Castle. The work was finished, however, in January, 1950, when everyone in Britain was being urged to contribute to the export drive, and Queen Mary decided to present her magnificent piece of work to the nation in order that it might be sold for dollars. Before leaving the country the carpet was exhibited at the Victoria and Albert Museum, where more than one hundred thousand people queued to see it. The only condition which she attached to the sale of the carpet, which was to go to the highest bidder, was that its eventual destination should be a public institution. It was thus acquired for the Canadian nation by the Imperial Order of Daughters of the Empire, and realized £35,354 18s., more than one hundred thousand dollars.

As soon as the war in Europe was over, and Marlborough House could be made ready for her occupation, Queen Mary returned to London. Her first post-war public engagement, on 10 July, 1945, when she visited one of the most cherished of her organizations, the London Hospital, marked the resumption of her normal active public life as one of London's most beloved citizens. Her proverbially good health endured, together with her excellent eyesight and her most acute sense of hearing. Her daily routine made few, if any, concessions to advancing years. She was still an early riser, always appearing fully dressed to take the first meal of the day in her breakfast room, before beginning her morning's work with the reading of the newspapers (or having these read aloud to her) and dealing with her large mail, either reading, or at least hearing read, every letter addressed to her.

If the entries in her diary have been fewer than in the days when she was Queen Consort, this has been not so much because she has been "doing less" as because she has been more free to plan her days as they came along, although there have been certain annual engagements which she has rarely missed. One is the British Industries Fair in London, which she has attended since its inauguration in 1919, always wearing the Number One badge which was presented to her on that occasion. In the course of the years her visits have, at a conservative estimate, involved her walking considerably more than one hundred miles, an achievement which no one else—either official or visitor—has ever ventured to claim. The Antique Dealers' Fair has been another of her favourite events to which she has almost always paid two visits, one on a Sunday, enabling her to examine the exhibits at leisure, and another on a weekday, to mix with

A HELPING HAND FOR QUEEN MARY

Willing hands help Queen Mary over the stepping-stones during a visit to the Chelsea Flower Show.

the general public. Her tour of the Chelsea Flower Show is equally thorough and she refuses to be daunted even when difficult walking is involved, merely accepting the offer of a guiding arm to give her a slight support over the stepping stones of the ornamental water.

Queen Mary's long stay in the country meant that she was largely deprived of one of the great pleasures of her life, the theatre. In the years immediately after the war she became a regular playgoer, sometimes seeing two, and even occasionally three, plays in a week. This has remained her favourite evening entertainment. When at home she listens to the nine o'clock news on the radio every night, and sometimes to a discussion or talk, while television, also installed at Marlborough House, has enabled her to "watch" interesting ceremonies at which she could not conveniently be present in person, but both of these modern forms of entertainment have appealed to her only in moderation.

Since the beginning of the war Queen Mary has never entertained on a large scale, but her return to London enabled her to resume her former custom of giving small parties for old friends and visiting relatives, and she often likes to have one or two guests to lunch. She appreciates good food and, although she both eats and drinks sparingly, she takes pleasure in providing her guests with a choice meal and excellent wines, despite rationing regulations, always scrupulously observed in her household.

Afternoon tea has always remained a favourite meal with her, and at this time of the day she often receives a guest with whom she wishes to enjoy a quiet hour's conversation. The pleasant ritual of serving tea in her home has changed little in half a century. A silver kettle is brought in, complete with its small spirit-stove, so that Queen Mary can supervise the brewing of her favourite beverage. She herself applies an old-fashioned extinguisher to the flame only after she has refilled the pot with really boiling water for the second cup. Toasted muffins are served, as these are a favourite delicacy with Queen Mary, who does not—even as an octogenarian—share the popular view that they are indigestible.

An eventful year for Queen Mary came in 1947. Her eightieth birthday on 26 May was followed, a few weeks later, by the announcement of the betrothal of the present Queen, who thus became the first of her grandchildren to marry. Throughout the preparations for the wedding Queen Mary's advice was constantly sought, as it had been on so many great family occasions in the past. She took much joy in admiring her

QUEEN MARY VISITS THE 1951 B.I.F.

Visiting the Olympia section, Queen Mary accepts a "ride" rather than miss any of the Fair.

granddaughter's hundreds of wedding presents and suggesting ways in which these could be used when the bride was able to set up house for herself. Queen Mary's proverbial memory, about which so many well-known stories have been told, is as remarkable today as it was forty years ago. Many of those who had sent wedding gifts were amazed when, on Queen Mary meeting them weeks or even months later, she referred to their present and the pleasure which it had given. More than a year after the wedding she happened to be talking to one of the doctors who, on behalf of a group of colleagues, had given a roll of white silk, and she remarked what a useful gift this had proved as it had provided her great-grandson with some of his first small garments.

Even Queen Mary has rarely received a more enthusiastic reception from Londoners than on the Sunday night in November, 1948, when she became a great-grandmother for the first time. Those who saw her arrive at Buckingham Palace, where the heir to the throne had just been born, waited a full hour to see her leave. It was close on midnight when they, and many others who had joined them outside the Palace gates, saw Queen Mary drive away, her car followed by cheering crowds who accompanied her right back to Marlborough House. Now that Prince Charles has been joined by Princess Anne yet another generation of the family is learning those first lessons in the royal way of life which Queen Mary taught her children half a century ago.

Already many small incidents have shown that the young heir to the throne, like his mother and grandfather before him, is responding at an early age in his training in royal courtesy. A few months before her accession the Queen was visiting the London food factory of one of the largest catering firms when she was presented with a wooden horse and cart for her little son. She was so impressed by what she had seen in her tour that she arranged for some of her own domestic staff to visit the premises, and as a result of this they invited several of the firm's employees to have tea with them at Clarence House. While the little tea-party was in progress the door opened and Prince Charles, who had learnt of their visit, came in to say his own "thank you" for his lovely toy.

Queen Mary has taken a great delight in choosing gifts for her great-grandchildren. Although many of her presents have been toys, she has also given them other possessions of more permanent value. When she learnt that a silver christening cup which had been presented by George III to one of his godsons was for sale she immediately purchased this for her own godson, young Prince Charles.

Looking back over the many public appearances which Queen Mary has made since she became a great-grandmother it is difficult to believe that she is already halfway through her ninth decade of life. Each year has seen her setting forth in search of new experiences. One day, in the late summer of 1949, found her taking tea in a Lambeth "pre-fab" whose occupier had won the cup which she herself gave for the best garden produced by a tenant of this extremely modern type of house. In the winter of the

AN INFORMAL VISIT TO THE THEATRE

In the years since the war Queen Mary has been able to indulge her love of the theatre. Here she arrives at the Fortune Theatre for a matinée performance of Agatha Christie's The Hollow.

following year Queen Mary endured one of her rare periods of ill health, for she was confined to her home with an attack of sciatica.

Her first public engagement after her recovery was a visit to the Royal School of Needlework on a bitter December day. When she left everyone was naturally anxious to see her warmly tucked up in her car, but Queen Mary has never taken kindly to being treated as a convalescent. Seeing two little boys clutching small boats, she paused to ask them if they were going to sail these in the Serpentine, and listened with interest as they explained that this was exactly what they had just been doing. The boys happened to be Americans and they returned to their home exuberant at this unexpected conversation with "the first Queen we'd ever seen."

No woman has ever grown old more gracefully than Queen Mary. It is no vain effort to belie her years, but rather the vitality of her mind, her great zest for living and her determination to know what is going on in the world around her which has led her to spurn the leisured existence of the arm-chair and fireside. Often the intimation that Queen Mary will be arriving on a tour of inspection of this or that causes consternation to those who hold less enlightened views on the capabilities of octogenarians. When she was in her eighty-third year Queen Mary heard that much interesting work had been undertaken to enhance the attraction of the famous armour display at the Tower of London—one of the historic buildings for which she has always had a special affection. When she announced that she proposed to inspect these improvements in person the authorities were greatly distressed, because the armoury could be reached only by a winding flight of one hundred and fifty-five awkward stone steps. A portable invalid chair was therefore obtained and stalwart members of the staff briefed to be on hand to carry it. Queen Mary, however, looked so sprightly when she arrived that no reference was made to this arrangement until she herself noticed the chair standing in readiness at the foot of the stairs and, pointing to it with her umbrella, inquired for whose use it was intended. She then mounted the stairs on foot at a steady pace which left her escorts thankful to pause for breath at the top.

It is only on exceptional occasions, when she is making a tour which would otherwise involve walking or standing for several hours at a stretch, that Queen Mary will gracefully admit that there is something to be said for a comfortable seat on wheels. When she visited the British Industries Fair at Olympia a week or two before her eighty-fourth birthday she waved away the attendants with the chair and for the first hour made her inspection on foot. Then she decided that, as there was still so much ground to be covered, she would "ride" the rest of the way rather than miss any of the exhibits or fail to give these her customary thorough inspection. For that was in 1951, a busy year for Queen Mary as for all her family, and only a few days earlier she had made a complete tour of the Festival of Britain Exhibition on the South Bank, an undertaking which daunted many people half her age. On this occasion, too, a wheeled chair came into requisition, but—lest anyone should suspect that Queen Mary was at

TEA IN A LONDON PRE-FAB

Queen Mary takes tea with Mr. William Mucklow, winner of the cup which she gave in 1949 for the best garden produced by the tenant of a pre-fab.

A GREAT-GRANDMOTHER FOR THE FIRST TIME

Queen Mary holds the month-old Prince Charles after the christening in December, 1948.

QUEEN MARY TOURS THE SOUTH BANK FESTIVAL EXHIBITION

Two of her grandsons, Prince Michael of Kent and Prince William of Gloucester, accompanied Queen Mary when she visited the South Bank and toured the exhibition with her usual thoroughness.

last resigning herself to the régime which the world expects of a great-grandmother three times over—a week later she set forth from her home after ten o'clock at night for a sight-seeing tour to enjoy the lights of London. After spending three-quarters of an hour at the Savoy Hotel watching the illuminations on the South Bank, she went on to admire the flood-lighting at St. Paul's Cathedral. To thousands of the foreign visitors who came to Britain in the Festival year "your wonderful Queen Mary" was not the least of the sights of London.

Throughout 1951 Queen Mary, as in past years, was to be seen out and about almost daily in the London that she loves and whose citizens return her love with an affection bestowed only upon those who truly belong to their capital city. When, in February, 1952, Britain and her Commonwealth of Nations mourned the passing of their King, the sympathy of the world went out to the three Queens to whom the

QUEEN MARY REOPENS ASSEMBLY HALL

Queen Mary is received by Dr. Geoffrey Fisher, Archbishop of Canterbury, when she reopens the Assembly Hall at Church House, Westminster. This had been almost totally destroyed by bombing.

H.M. QUEEN MARY

Age has not lessened Queen Mary's grace and dignity, nor her interest in the welfare of her country and the life of its ordinary citizens. Universally beloved—and nowhere more than in her native London—Queen Mary receives a great welcome whenever she appears in public. This picture was taken as she drove out from Marlborough House on the eve of her eighty-fifth birthday.

Sovereign had been also father, husband and son. Once again the veteran Queen, who has survived not only most of her contemporaries but also two of her three younger brothers and three of her six children, set an example of serene and faithful courage to a sorrowing people.

Now the new reign has begun and, for the first time in the story of a monarchy which goes back a thousand years and more, one who has shared the Sovereign's throne as Consort has lived to see her granddaughter proclaimed as Queen. Queen Mary, who has helped to make so much of British history, remains close beside the new young Queen Elizabeth the Second, ready to give counsel from the rich storehouse of her memory as preparations move forward for that great ceremony which the eighty-five-year-old Queen has already witnessed three times over, the Coronation of a British Sovereign.

INDEX

ACKNOWLEDGEMENTS

Painting by J. Lavery, by courtesy of the National Portrait Gallery.
Painting by Solomon J. Solomon, by courtesy of the Guildhall Art Gallery.
Painting by Frank O. Salisbury, by courtesy of the Guildhall Art Gallery.